Plane spotting
Log book

This book belongs to :

Adresse

· ·

· ·

· ·

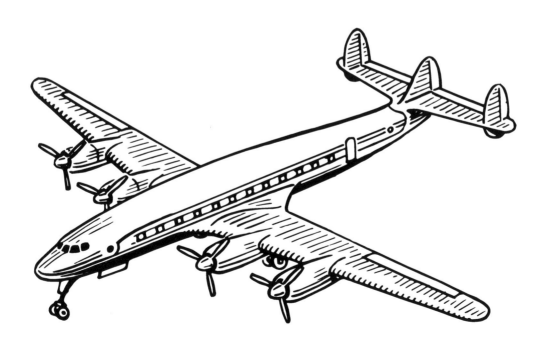

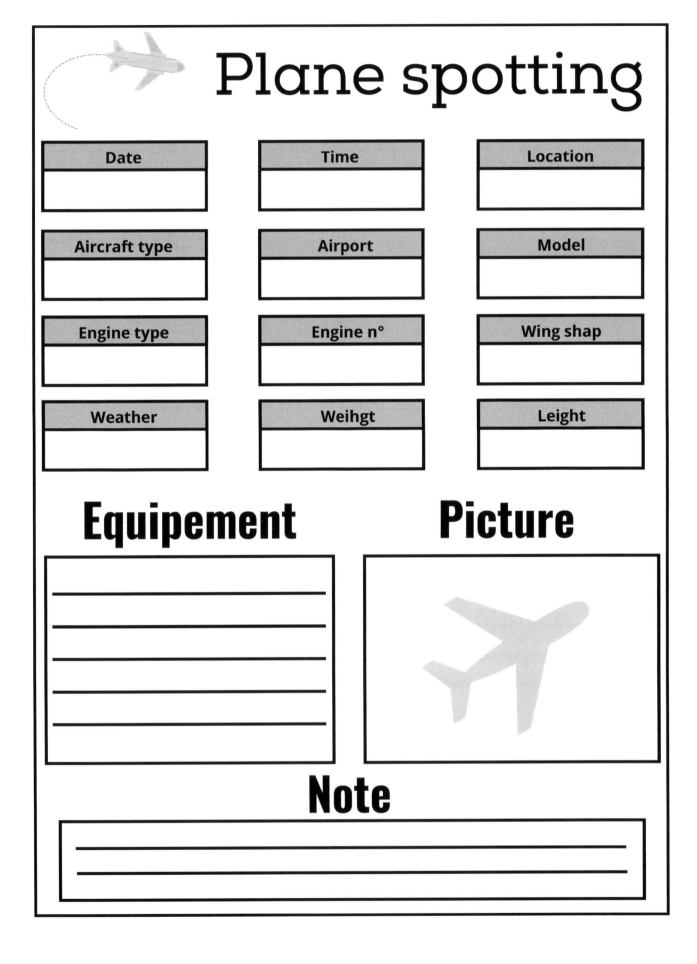

Plane spotting

Date	Time	Location

Aircraft type	Airport	Model

Engine type	Engine n°	Wing shap

Weather	Weihgt	Leight

Equipement

Picture

Note

Plane spotting

Date	Time	Location

Aircraft type	Airport	Model

Engine type	Engine n°	Wing shap

Weather	Weihgt	Leight

Equipement

Picture

Note

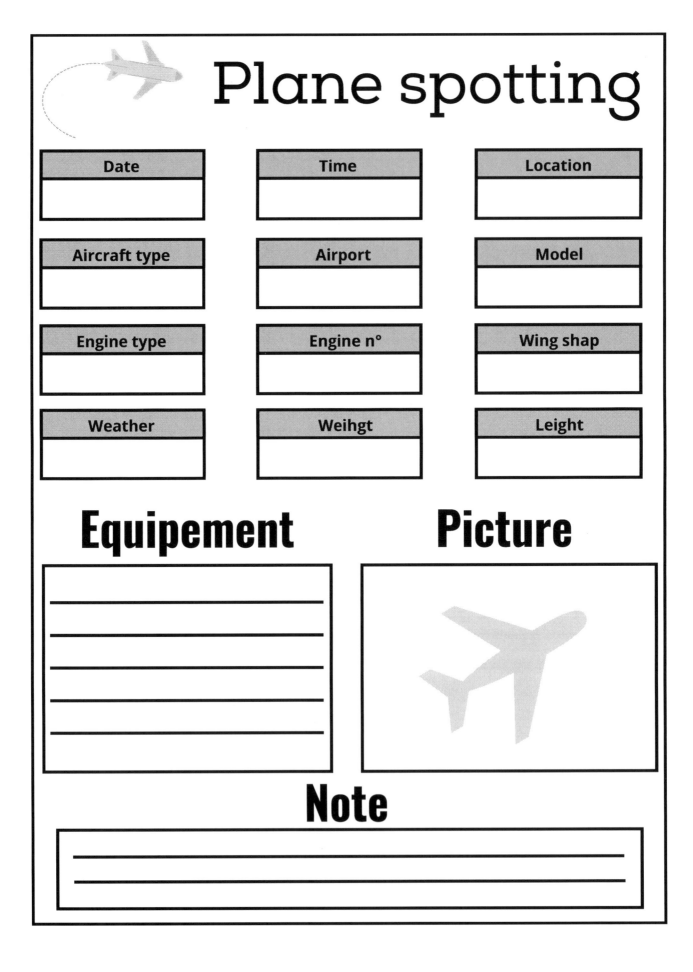

Plane spotting

Date	Time	Location

Aircraft type	Airport	Model

Engine type	Engine n°	Wing shap

Weather	Weihgt	Leight

Equipement

Picture

Note

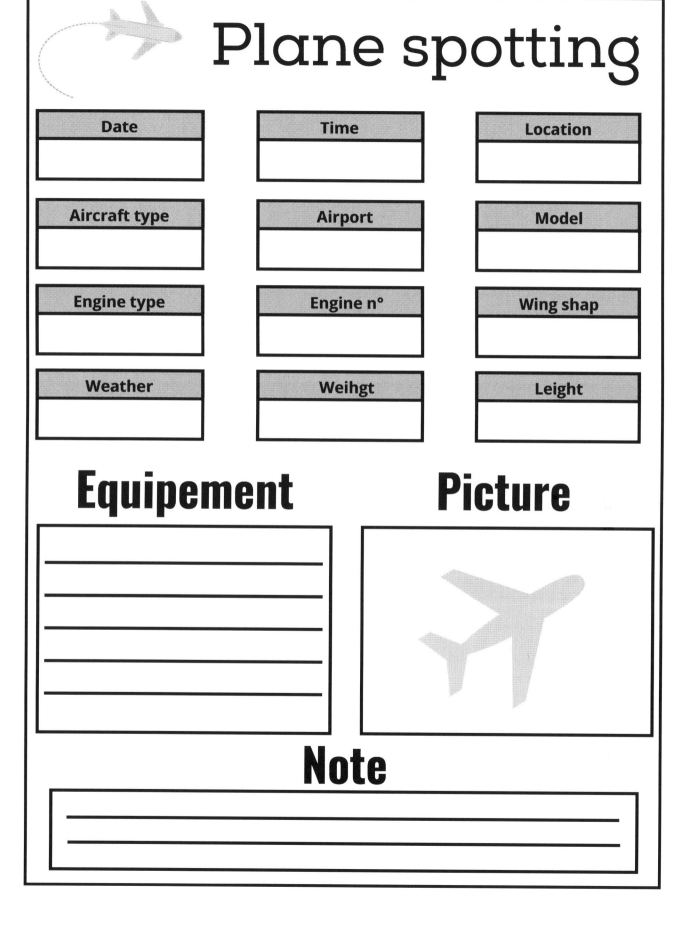

Plane spotting

Date	Time	Location

Aircraft type	Airport	Model

Engine type	Engine n°	Wing shap

Weather	Weihgt	Leight

Equipement

Picture

Note

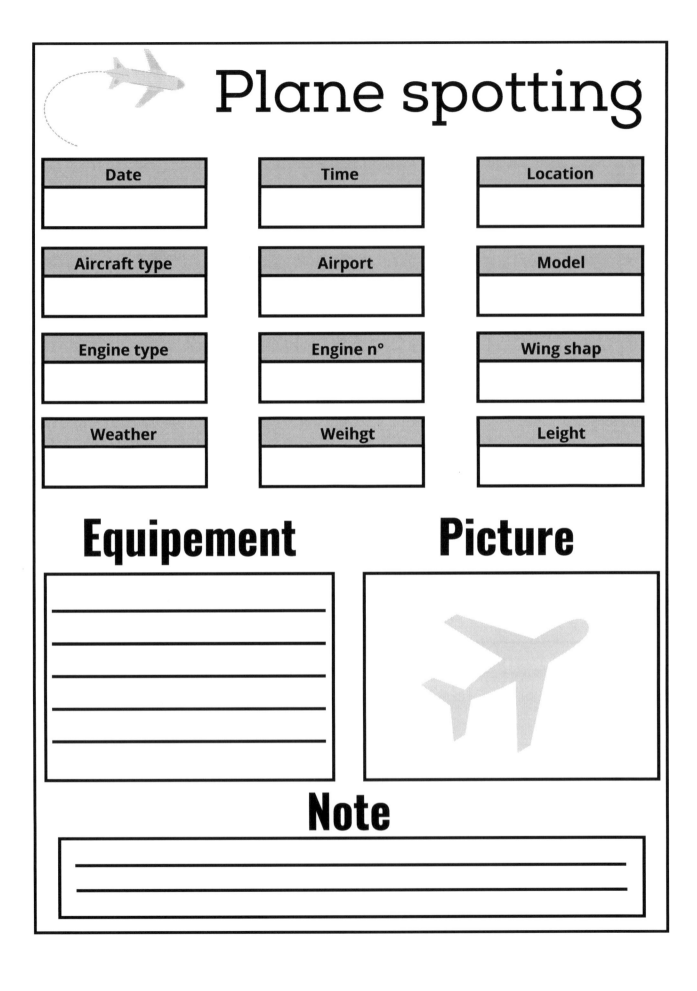

Plane spotting

Date	Time	Location

Aircraft type	Airport	Model

Engine type	Engine n°	Wing shap

Weather	Weihgt	Leight

Equipement

Picture

Note

Plane spotting

Date	Time	Location

Aircraft type	Airport	Model

Engine type	Engine n°	Wing shap

Weather	Weihgt	Leight

Equipement

Picture

Note

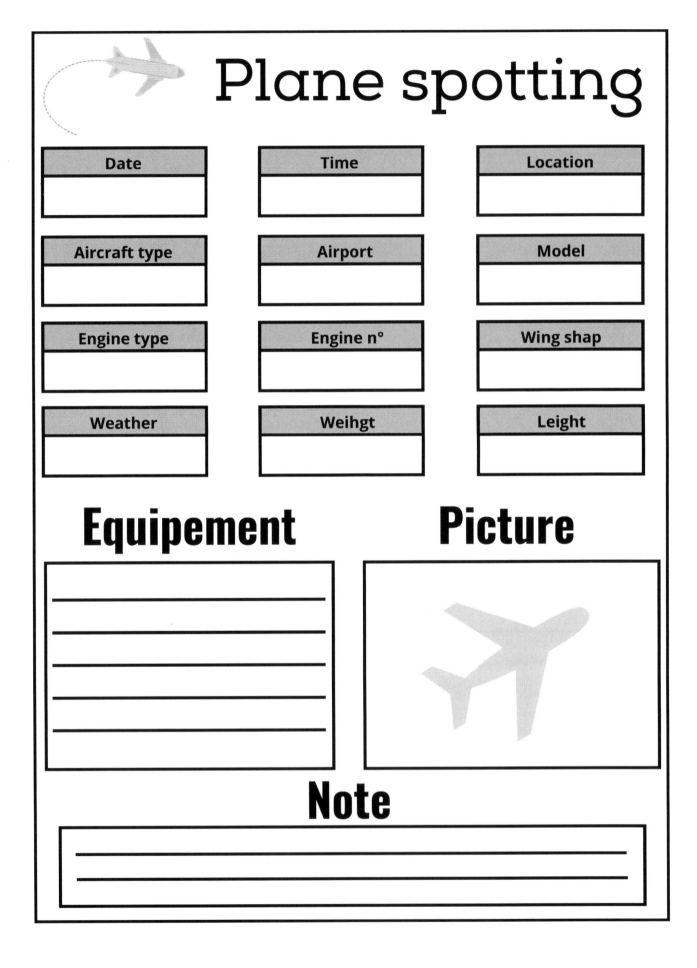

Plane spotting

Date	Time	Location

Aircraft type	Airport	Model

Engine type	Engine n°	Wing shap

Weather	Weihgt	Leight

Equipement

Picture

Note

Plane spotting

Date	Time	Location

Aircraft type	Airport	Model

Engine type	Engine n°	Wing shap

Weather	Weihgt	Leight

Equipement

Picture

Note

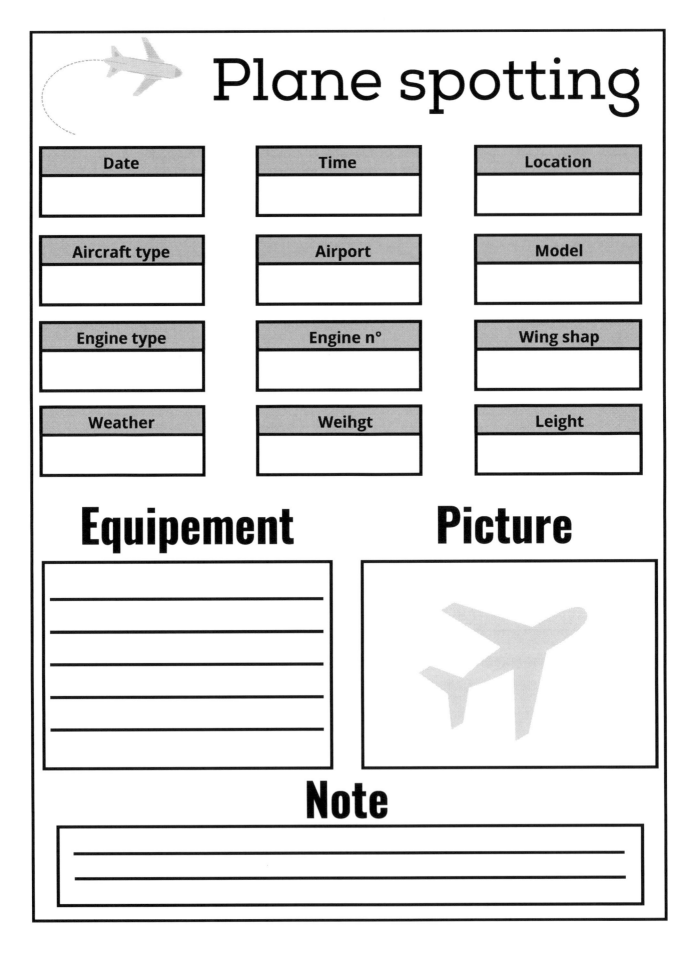

Plane spotting

Date	Time	Location

Aircraft type	Airport	Model

Engine type	Engine n°	Wing shap

Weather	Weihgt	Leight

Equipement

Picture

Note

Plane spotting

Date	Time	Location

Aircraft type	Airport	Model

Engine type	Engine n°	Wing shap

Weather	Weihgt	Leight

Equipement

Picture

Note

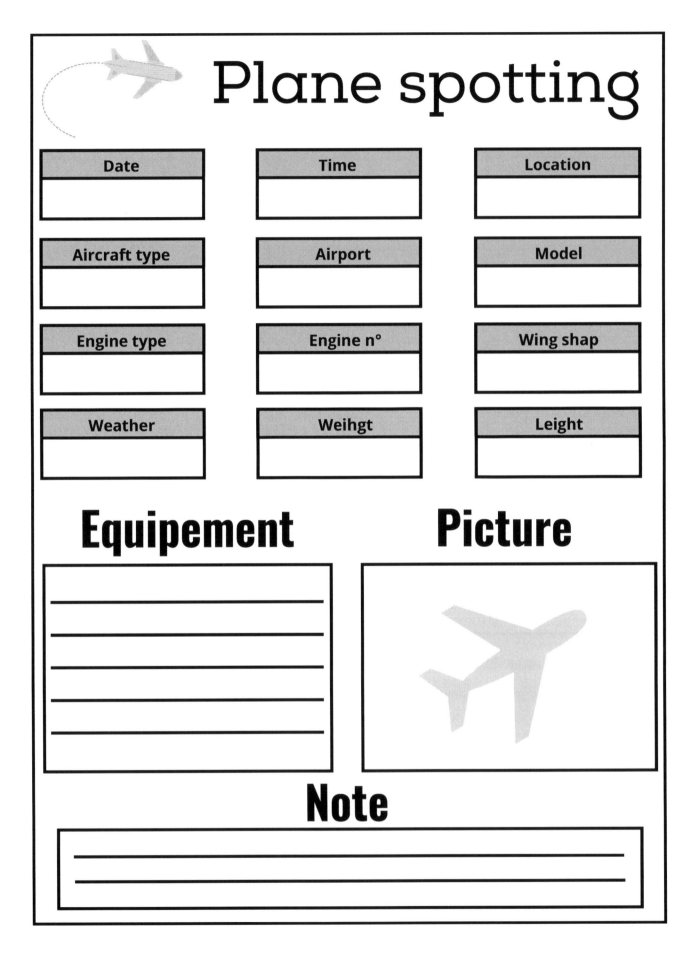

Plane spotting

Date	Time	Location

Aircraft type	Airport	Model

Engine type	Engine n°	Wing shap

Weather	Weihgt	Leight

Equipement

Picture

Note

Plane spotting

Date	Time	Location

Aircraft type	Airport	Model

Engine type	Engine n°	Wing shap

Weather	Weihgt	Leight

Equipement

Picture

Note

Plane spotting

Date	Time	Location

Aircraft type	Airport	Model

Engine type	Engine n°	Wing shap

Weather	Weihgt	Leight

Equipement

Picture

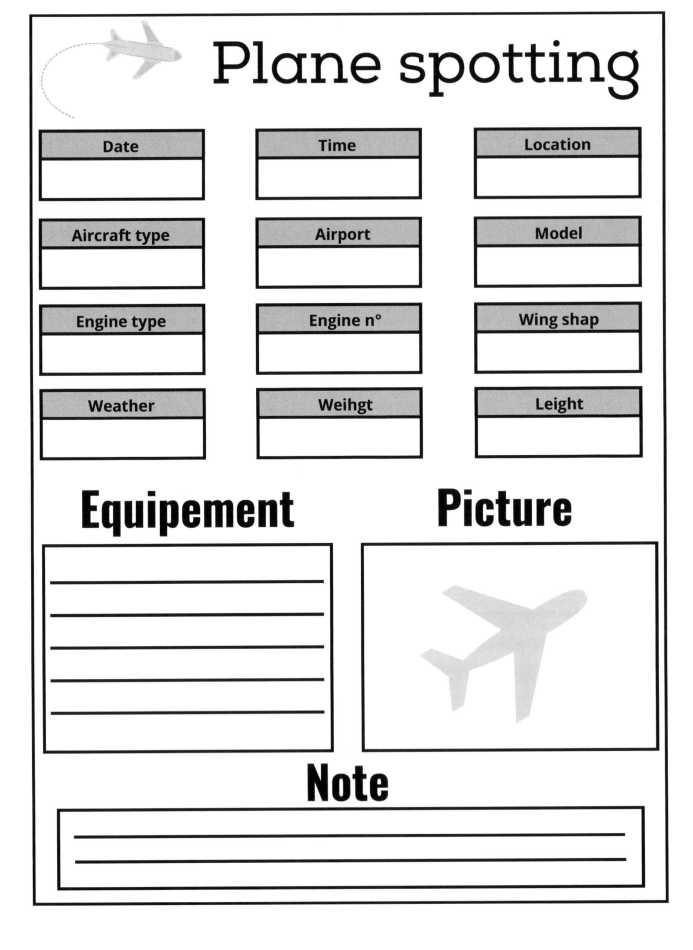

Note

Plane spotting

Date	Time	Location

Aircraft type	Airport	Model

Engine type	Engine n°	Wing shap

Weather	Weihgt	Leight

Equipement

Picture

Note

Plane spotting

Date	Time	Location

Aircraft type	Airport	Model

Engine type	Engine n°	Wing shap

Weather	Weihgt	Leight

Equipement

Picture

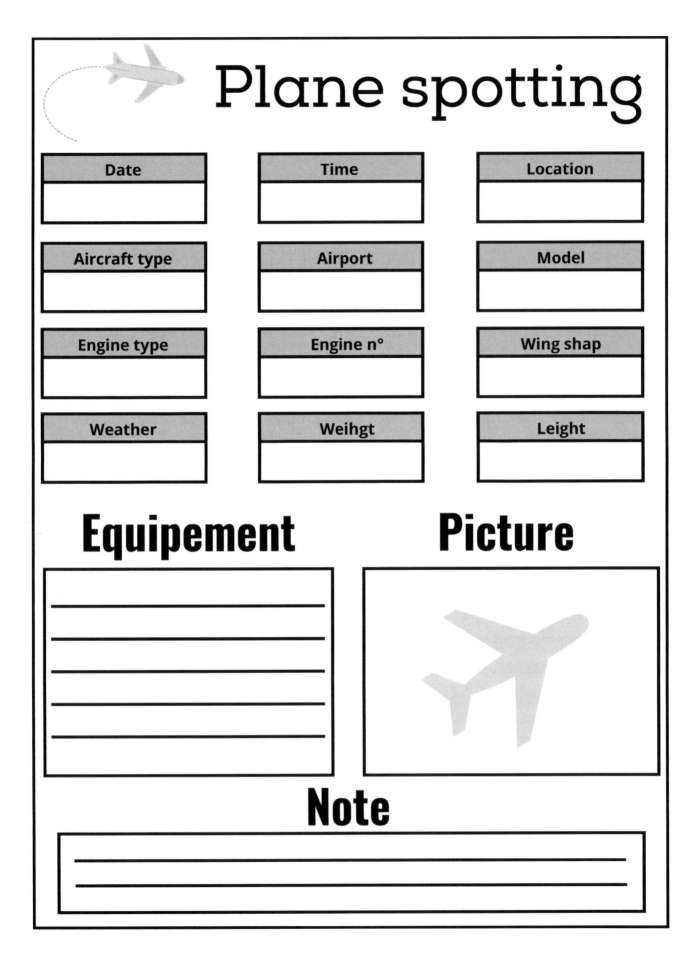

Note

Plane spotting

Date	Time	Location

Aircraft type	Airport	Model

Engine type	Engine n°	Wing shap

Weather	Weihgt	Leight

Equipement

Picture

Note

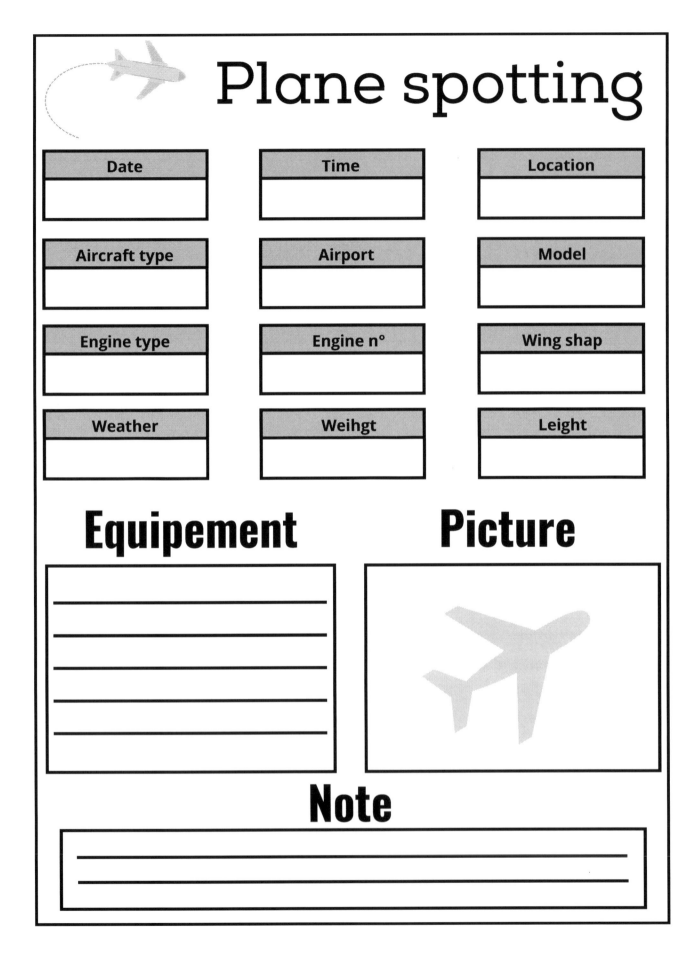

Plane spotting

Date	Time	Location

Aircraft type	Airport	Model

Engine type	Engine n°	Wing shap

Weather	Weihgt	Leight

Equipement

Picture

Note

Plane spotting

Date	Time	Location

Aircraft type	Airport	Model

Engine type	Engine n°	Wing shap

Weather	Weihgt	Leight

Equipement

Picture

Note

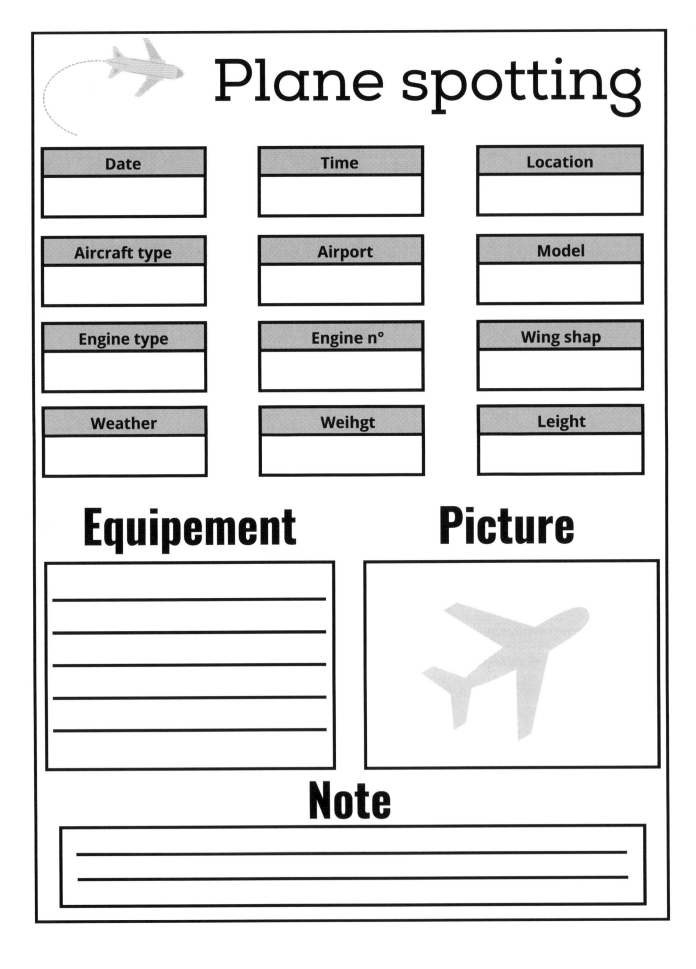

Plane spotting

Date	Time	Location

Aircraft type	Airport	Model

Engine type	Engine n°	Wing shap

Weather	Weihgt	Leight

Equipement

Picture

Note

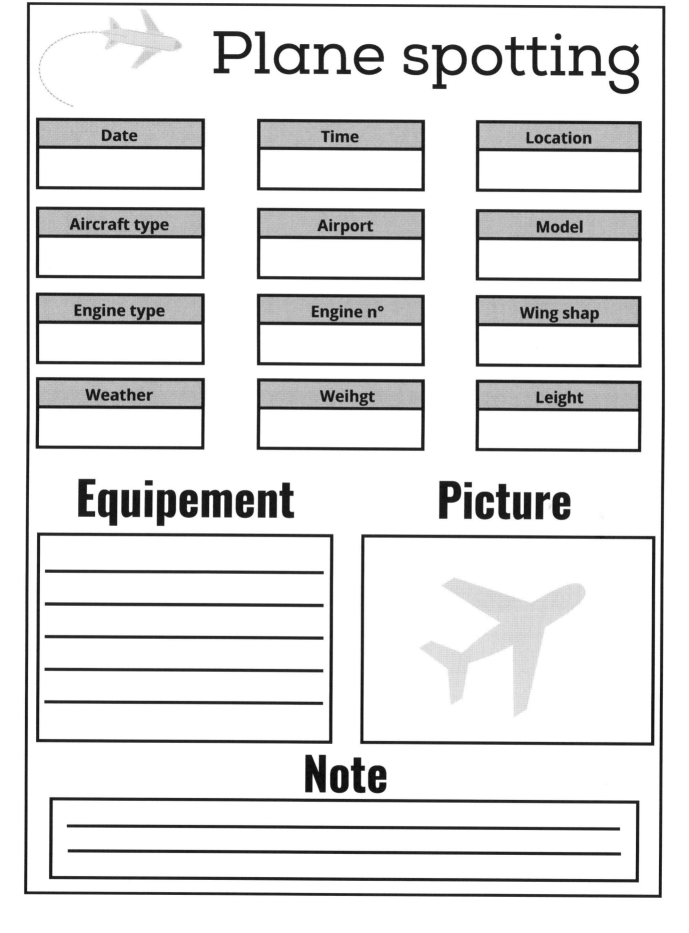

Plane spotting

Date	Time	Location

Aircraft type	Airport	Model

Engine type	Engine n°	Wing shap

Weather	Weihgt	Leight

Equipement

Picture

Note

Plane spotting

Date	Time	Location

Aircraft type	Airport	Model

Engine type	Engine n°	Wing shap

Weather	Weihgt	Leight

Equipement

Picture

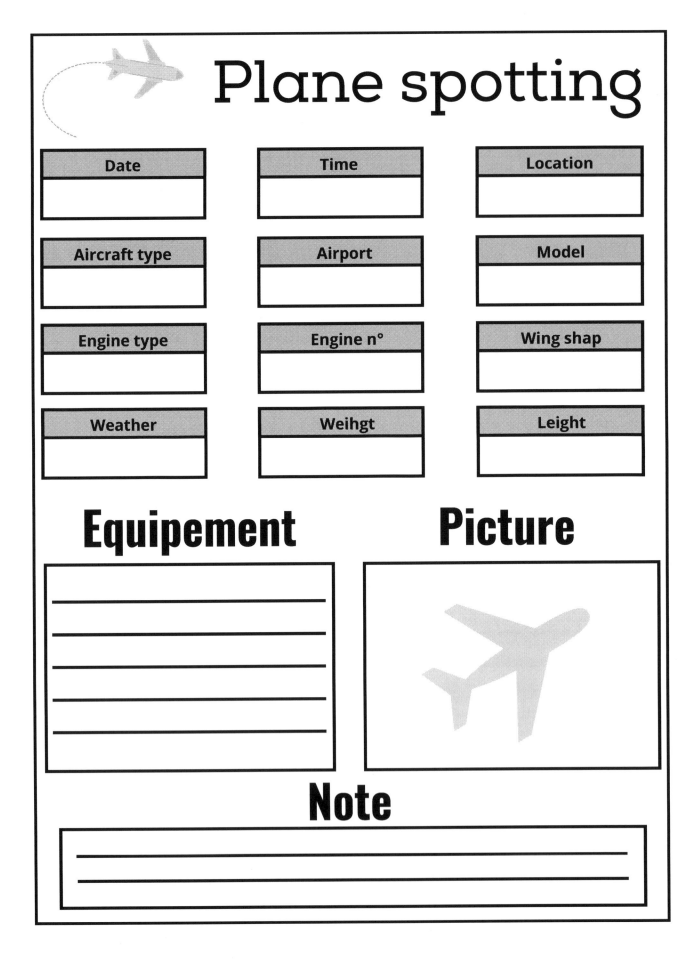

Note

Plane spotting

Date	Time	Location

Aircraft type	Airport	Model

Engine type	Engine n°	Wing shap

Weather	Weihgt	Leight

Equipement

Picture

Note

Plane spotting

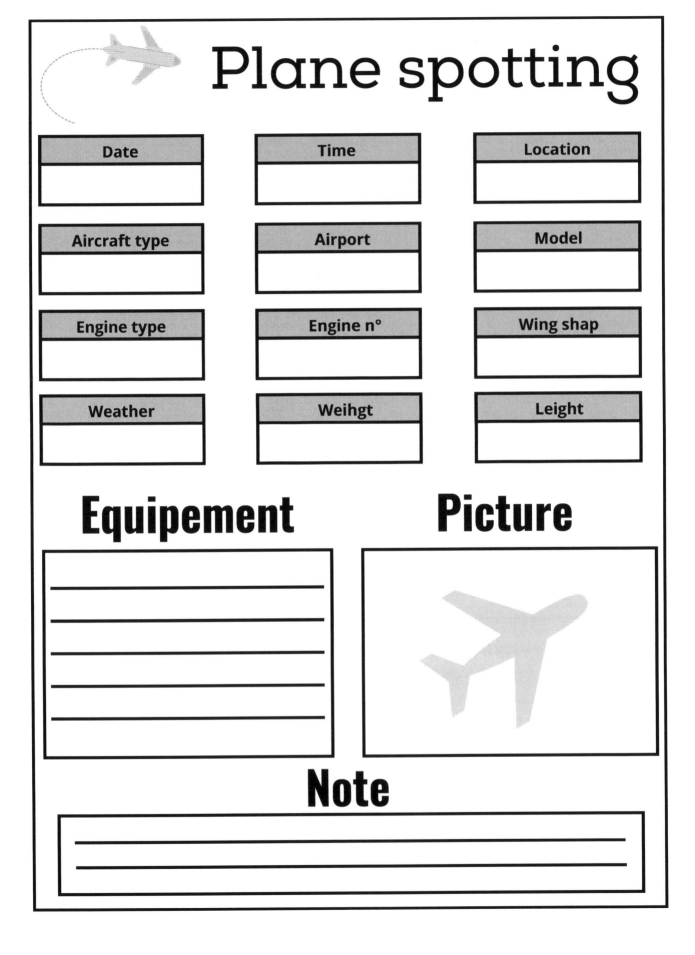

Date	Time	Location

Aircraft type	Airport	Model

Engine type	Engine n°	Wing shap

Weather	Weihgt	Leight

Equipement

Picture

Note

Plane spotting

Date	Time	Location

Aircraft type	Airport	Model

Engine type	Engine n°	Wing shap

Weather	Weihgt	Leight

Equipement

Picture

Note

Plane spotting

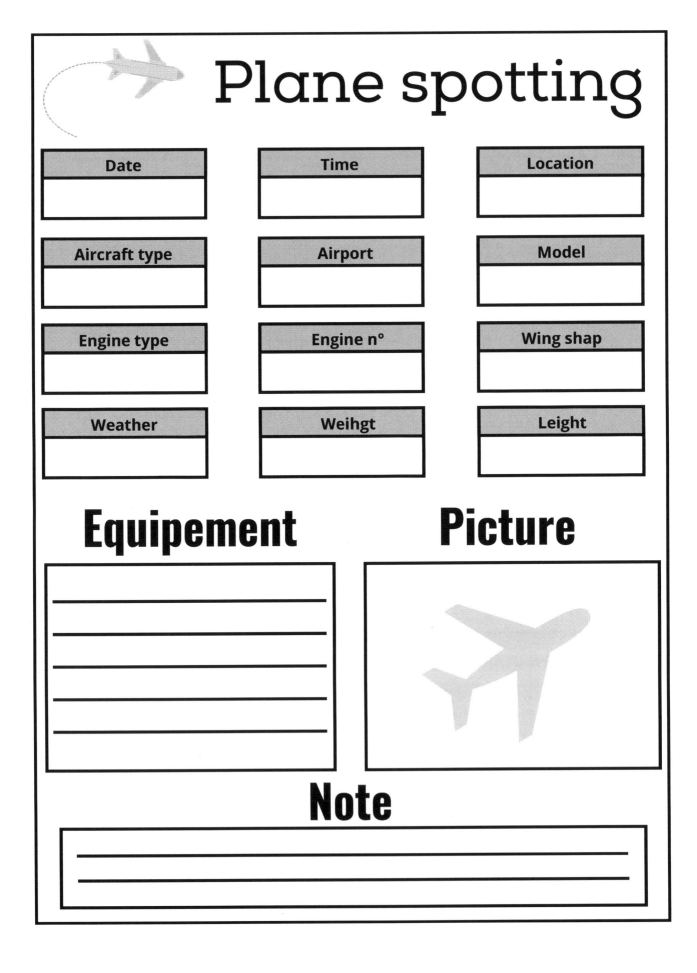

Date	Time	Location

Aircraft type	Airport	Model

Engine type	Engine n°	Wing shap

Weather	Weihgt	Leight

Equipement

Picture

Note

Plane spotting

Date	Time	Location

Aircraft type	Airport	Model

Engine type	Engine n°	Wing shap

Weather	Weihgt	Leight

Equipement

Picture

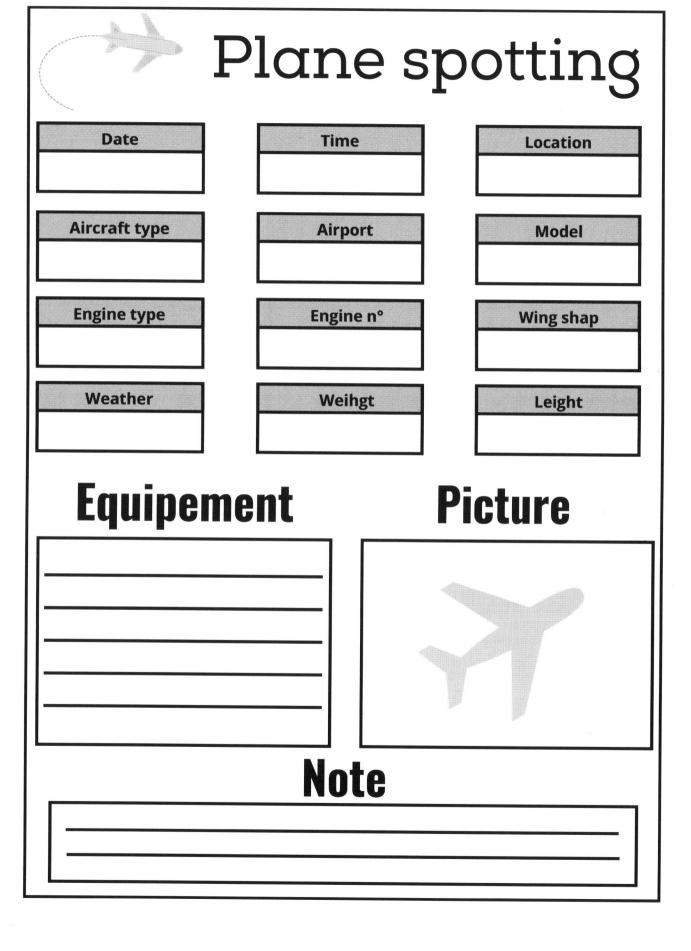

Note

Plane spotting

Date	Time	Location

Aircraft type	Airport	Model

Engine type	Engine n°	Wing shap

Weather	Weihgt	Leight

Equipement

Picture

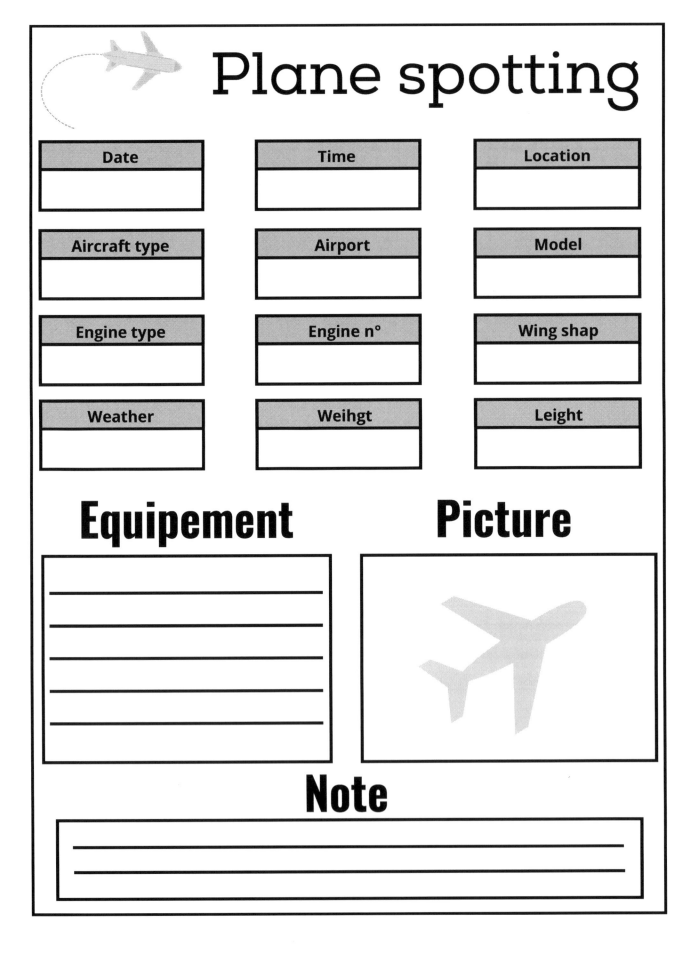

Note

Plane spotting

Date	Time	Location

Aircraft type	Airport	Model

Engine type	Engine n°	Wing shap

Weather	Weihgt	Leight

Equipement

Picture

Note

Plane spotting

Date	Time	Location

Aircraft type	Airport	Model

Engine type	Engine n°	Wing shap

Weather	Weihgt	Leight

Equipement

Picture

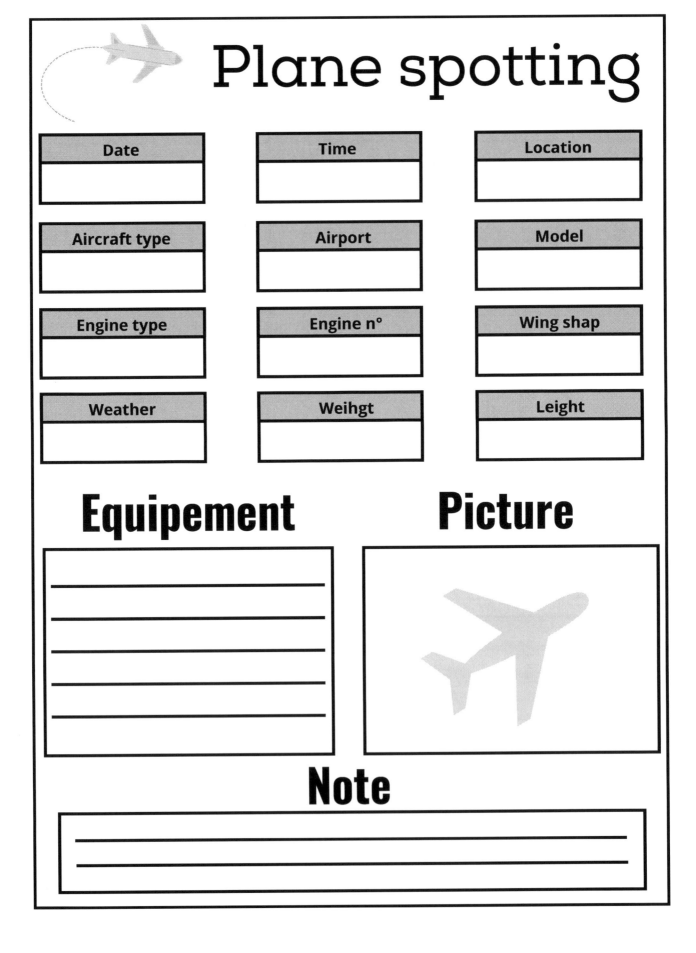

Note

Plane spotting

Date	Time	Location

Aircraft type	Airport	Model

Engine type	Engine n°	Wing shap

Weather	Weihgt	Leight

Equipement

Picture

Note

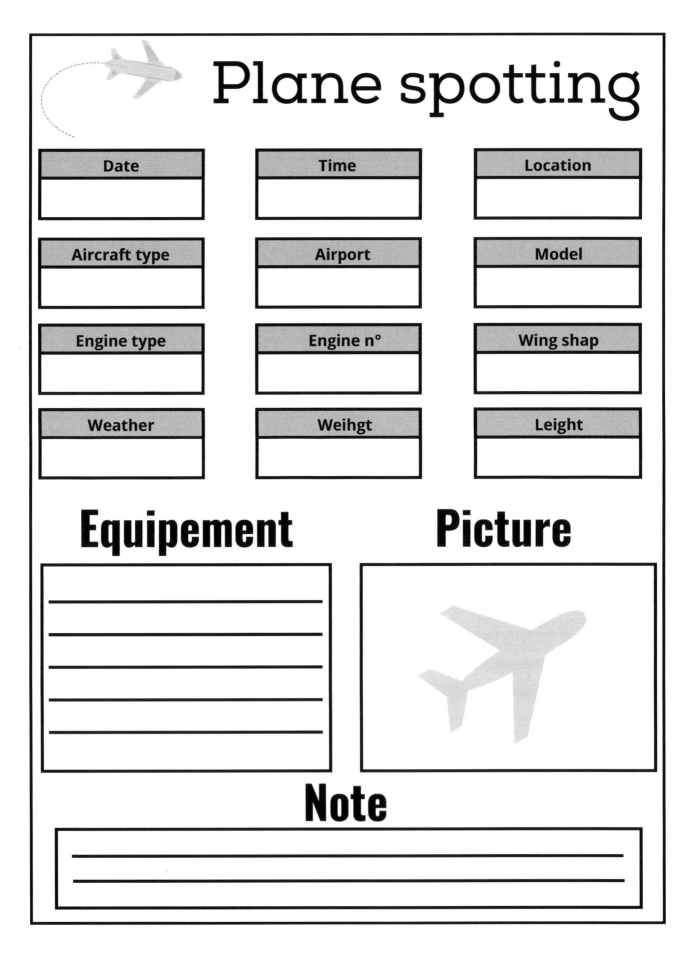

Plane spotting

Date	Time	Location

Aircraft type	Airport	Model

Engine type	Engine n°	Wing shap

Weather	Weihgt	Leight

Equipement

Picture

Note

Plane spotting

Date	Time	Location

Aircraft type	Airport	Model

Engine type	Engine n°	Wing shap

Weather	Weihgt	Leight

Equipement

Picture

Note

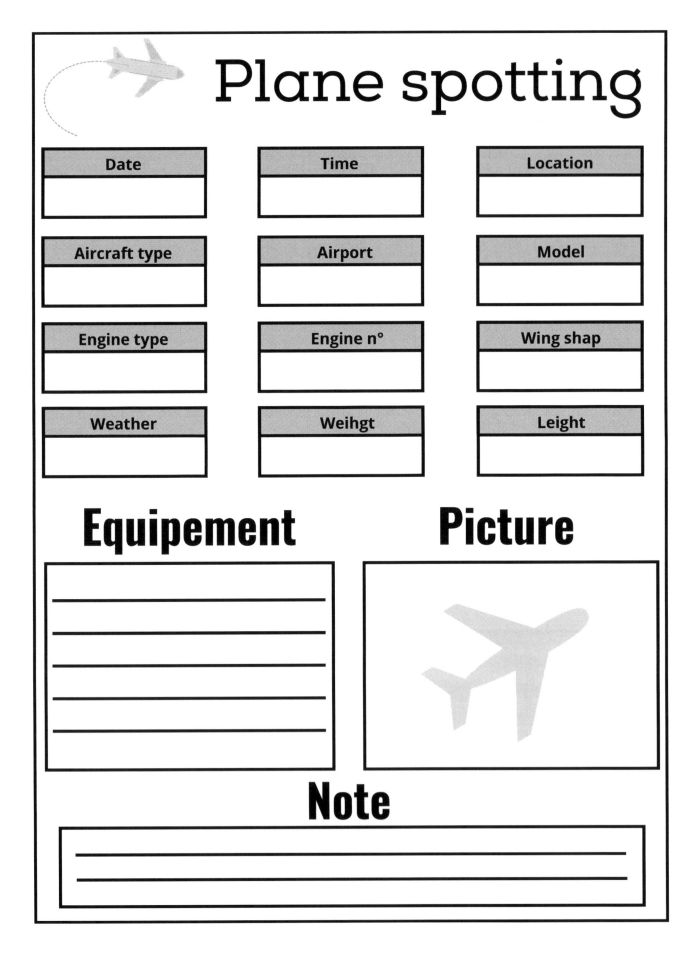

Plane spotting

Date	Time	Location

Aircraft type	Airport	Model

Engine type	Engine n°	Wing shap

Weather	Weihgt	Leight

Equipement

Picture

Note

Plane spotting

Date	Time	Location

Aircraft type	Airport	Model

Engine type	Engine n°	Wing shap

Weather	Weihgt	Leight

Equipement

Picture

Note

Plane spotting

Date	Time	Location

Aircraft type	Airport	Model

Engine type	Engine n°	Wing shap

Weather	Weihgt	Leight

Equipement

Picture

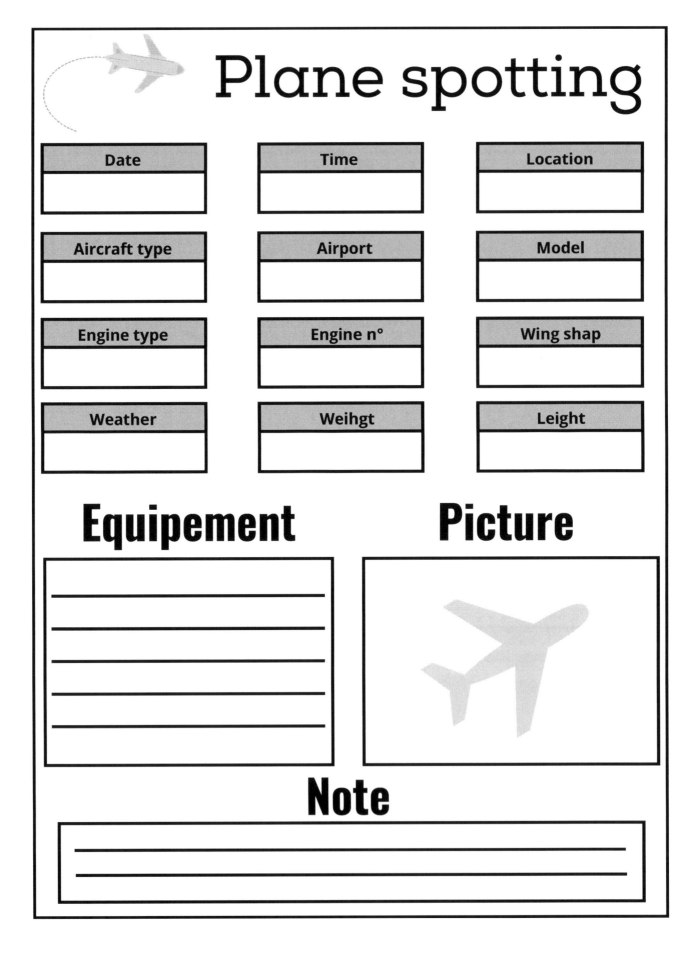

Note

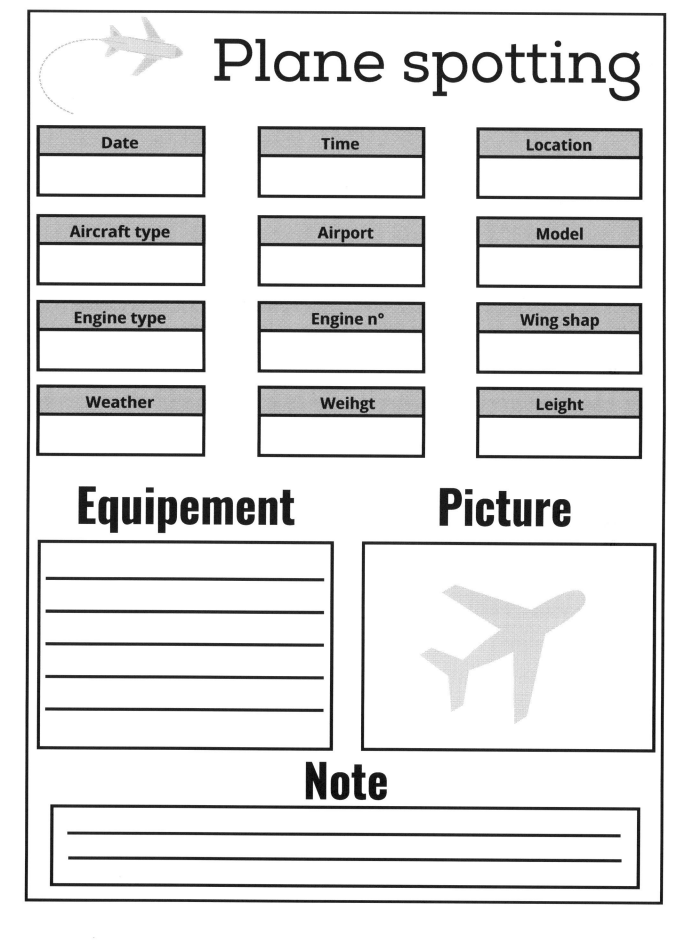

Plane spotting

Date	Time	Location

Aircraft type	Airport	Model

Engine type	Engine n°	Wing shap

Weather	Weihgt	Leight

Equipement

Picture

Note

Plane spotting

Date	Time	Location

Aircraft type	Airport	Model

Engine type	Engine n°	Wing shap

Weather	Weihgt	Leight

Equipement

Picture

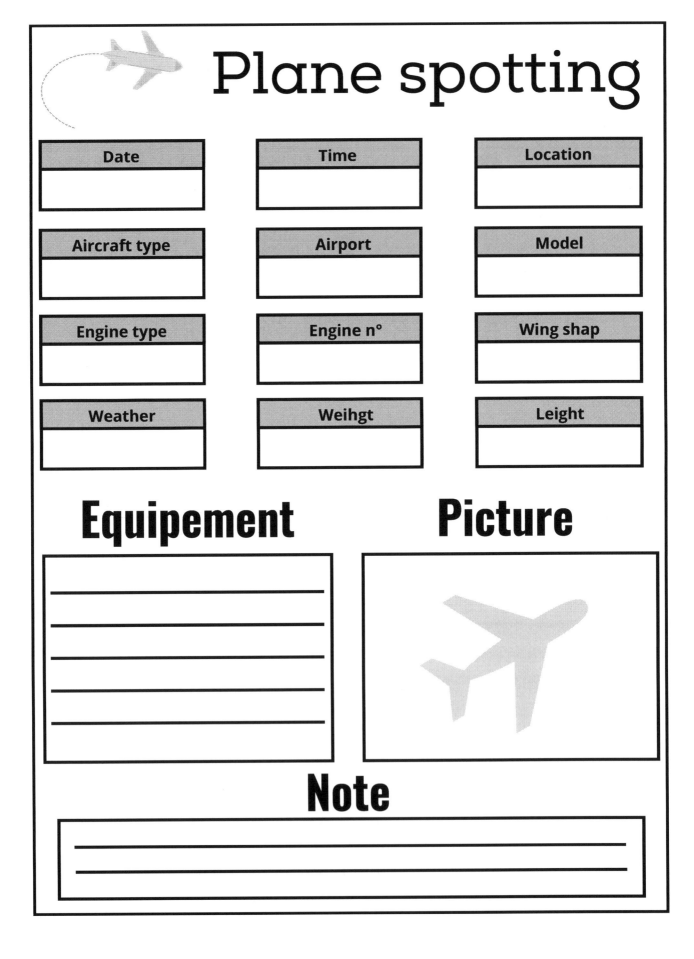

Note

Plane spotting

Date	Time	Location

Aircraft type	Airport	Model

Engine type	Engine n°	Wing shap

Weather	Weihgt	Leight

Equipement

Picture

Note

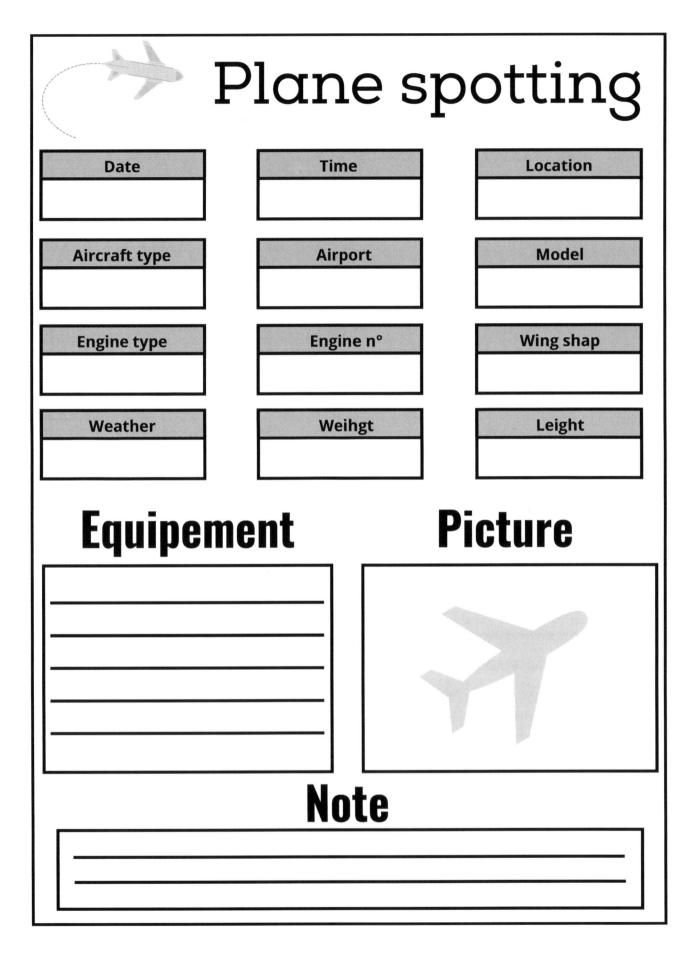

Plane spotting

Date	Time	Location

Aircraft type	Airport	Model

Engine type	Engine n°	Wing shap

Weather	Weihgt	Leight

Equipement

Picture

Note

Plane spotting

Date	Time	Location

Aircraft type	Airport	Model

Engine type	Engine n°	Wing shap

Weather	Weihgt	Leight

Equipement

Picture

Note

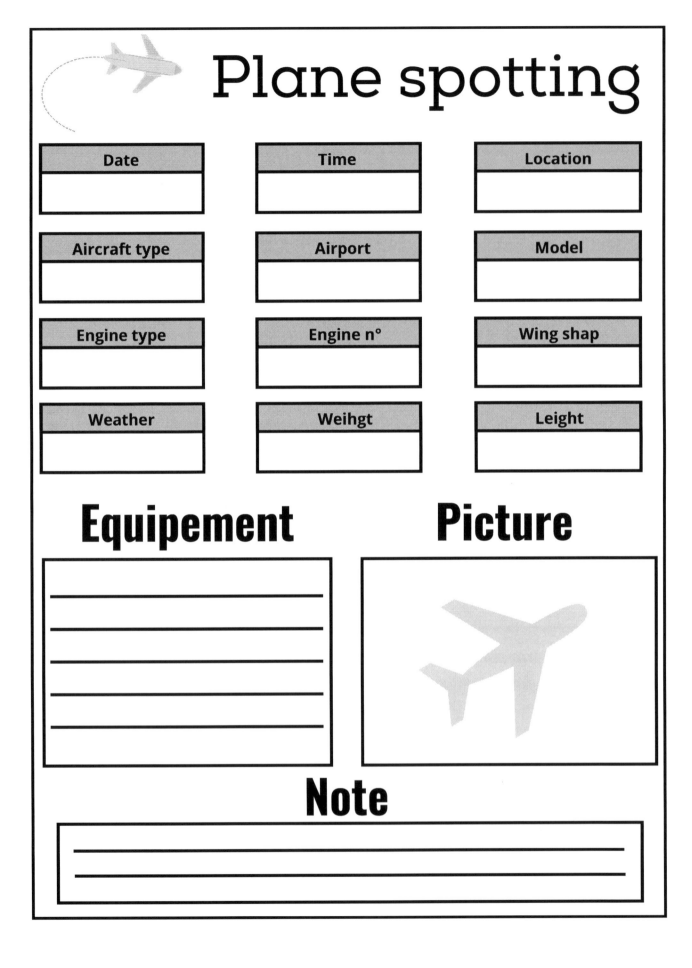

Plane spotting

Date	Time	Location

Aircraft type	Airport	Model

Engine type	Engine n°	Wing shap

Weather	Weihgt	Leight

Equipement

Picture

Note

Plane spotting

Date	Time	Location

Aircraft type	Airport	Model

Engine type	Engine n°	Wing shap

Weather	Weihgt	Leight

Equipement

Picture

Note

Plane spotting

Date	Time	Location

Aircraft type	Airport	Model

Engine type	Engine n°	Wing shap

Weather	Weihgt	Leight

Equipement

Picture

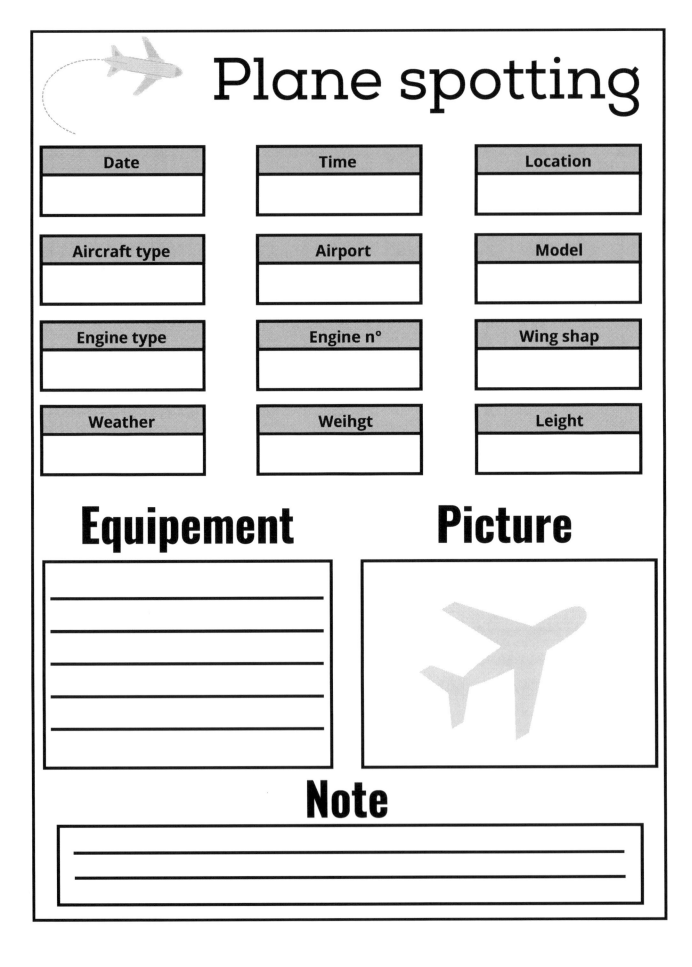

Note

Plane spotting

Date	Time	Location

Aircraft type	Airport	Model

Engine type	Engine n°	Wing shap

Weather	Weihgt	Leight

Equipement

Picture

Note

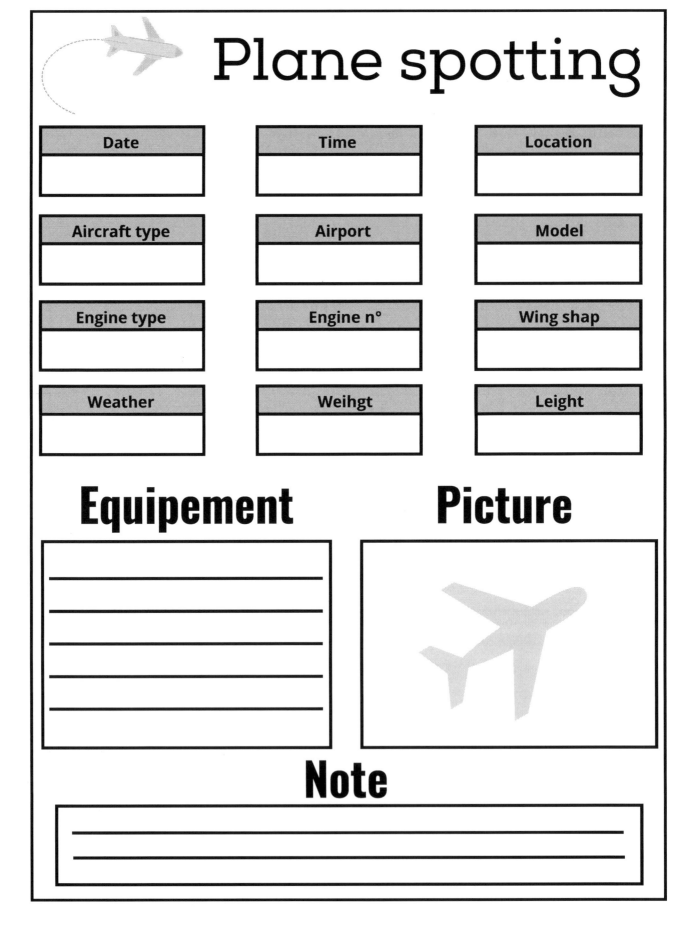

Plane spotting

Date	Time	Location

Aircraft type	Airport	Model

Engine type	Engine n°	Wing shap

Weather	Weihgt	Leight

Equipement

Picture

Note

Plane spotting

Date	Time	Location

Aircraft type	Airport	Model

Engine type	Engine n°	Wing shap

Weather	Weihgt	Leight

Equipement

Picture

Note

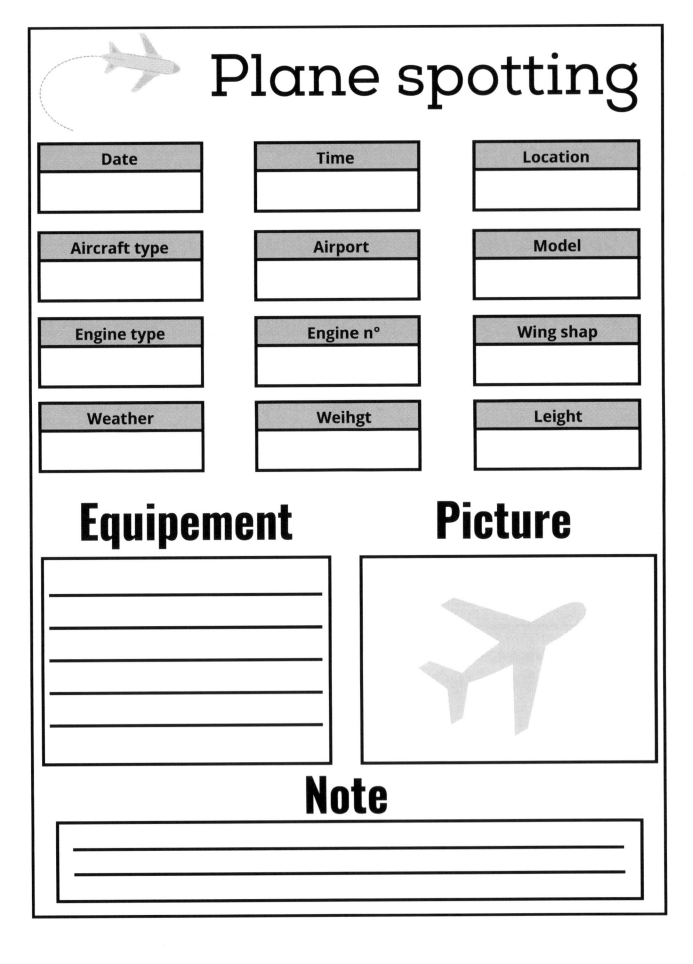

Plane spotting

Date	Time	Location

Aircraft type	Airport	Model

Engine type	Engine n°	Wing shap

Weather	Weihgt	Leight

Equipement

Picture

Note

Plane spotting

Date	Time	Location

Aircraft type	Airport	Model

Engine type	Engine n°	Wing shap

Weather	Weihgt	Leight

Equipement

Picture

Note

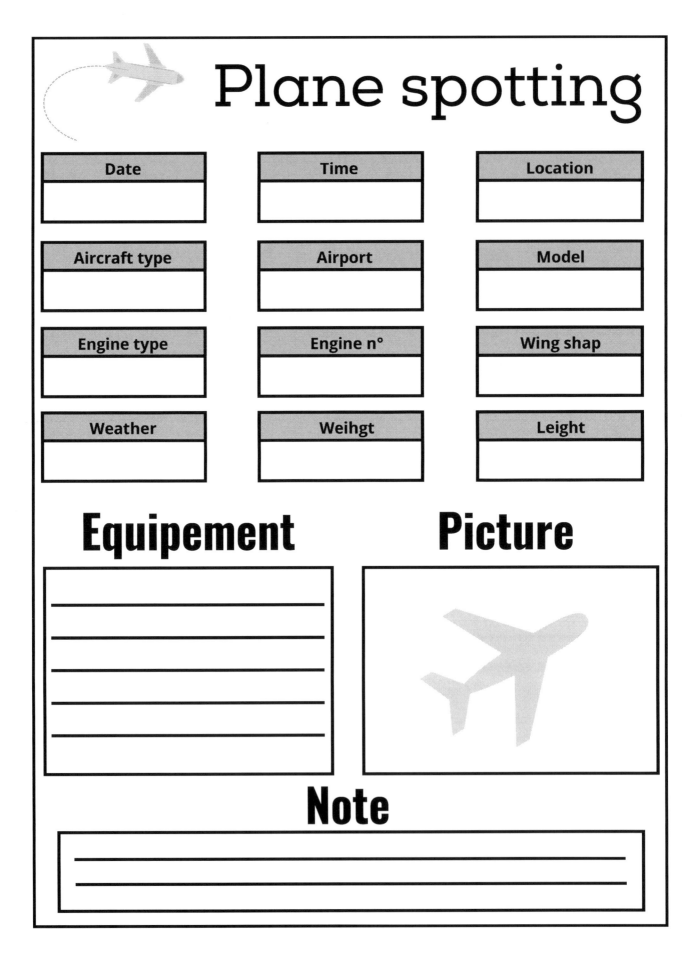

Plane spotting

Date	Time	Location

Aircraft type	Airport	Model

Engine type	Engine n°	Wing shap

Weather	Weihgt	Leight

Equipement

Picture

Note

Plane spotting

Date	Time	Location

Aircraft type	Airport	Model

Engine type	Engine n°	Wing shap

Weather	Weihgt	Leight

Equipement

Picture

Note

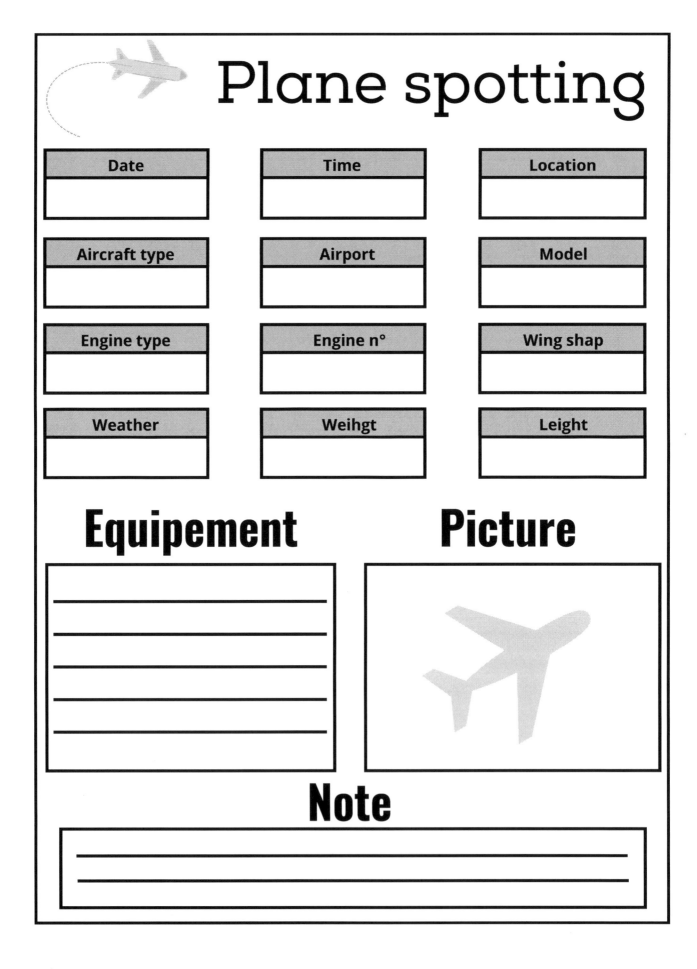

Plane spotting

Date	Time	Location

Aircraft type	Airport	Model

Engine type	Engine n°	Wing shap

Weather	Weihgt	Leight

Equipement

Picture

Note

Plane spotting

Date	Time	Location

Aircraft type	Airport	Model

Engine type	Engine n°	Wing shap

Weather	Weihgt	Leight

Equipement

Picture

Note

Plane spotting

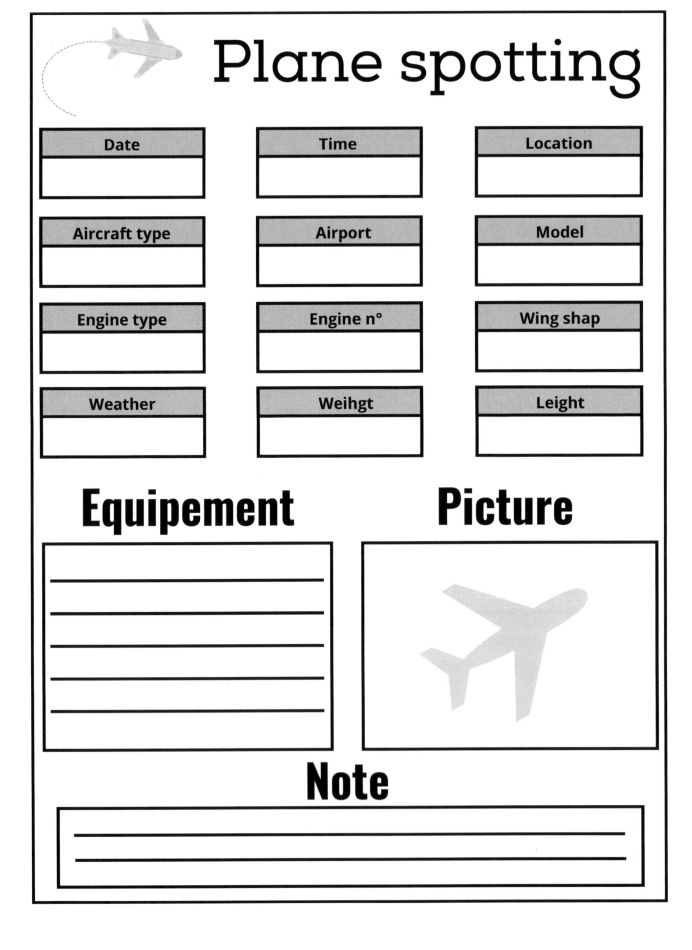

Date	Time	Location

Aircraft type	Airport	Model

Engine type	Engine n°	Wing shap

Weather	Weihgt	Leight

Equipement

Picture

Note

Plane spotting

Date	Time	Location

Aircraft type	Airport	Model

Engine type	Engine n°	Wing shap

Weather	Weihgt	Leight

Equipement

Picture

Note

Plane spotting

Date	Time	Location

Aircraft type	Airport	Model

Engine type	Engine n°	Wing shap

Weather	Weihgt	Leight

Equipement

Picture

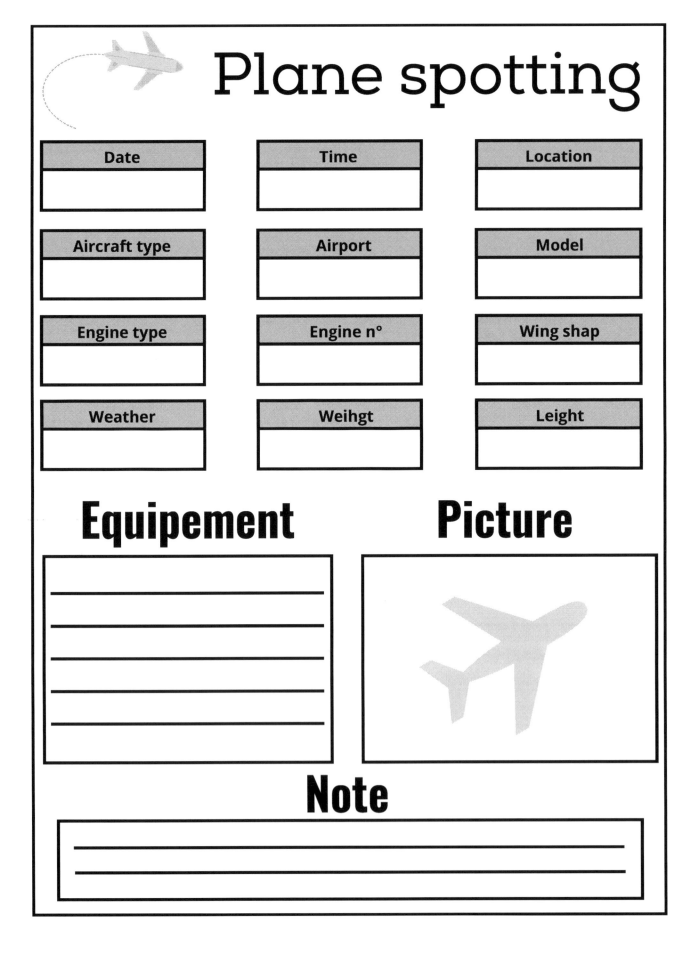

Note

Plane spotting

Date	Time	Location

Aircraft type	Airport	Model

Engine type	Engine n°	Wing shap

Weather	Weihgt	Leight

Equipement

Picture

Note

Plane spotting

Date	Time	Location

Aircraft type	Airport	Model

Engine type	Engine n°	Wing shap

Weather	Weihgt	Leight

Equipement

Picture

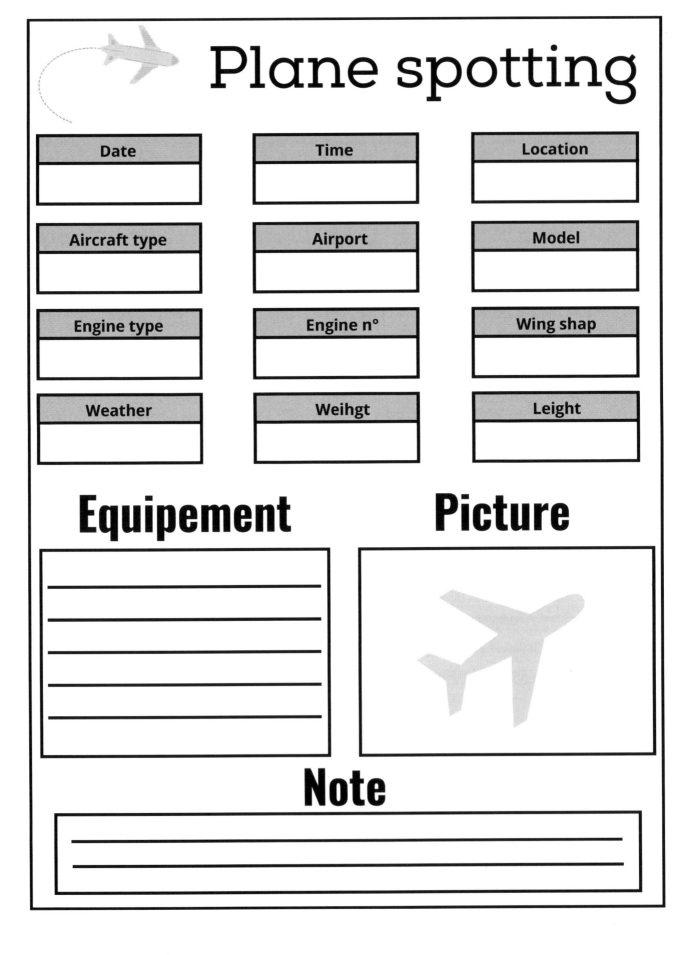

Note

Plane spotting

Date	Time	Location

Aircraft type	Airport	Model

Engine type	Engine n°	Wing shap

Weather	Weihgt	Leight

Equipement

Picture

Note

Plane spotting

Date	Time	Location

Aircraft type	Airport	Model

Engine type	Engine n°	Wing shap

Weather	Weihgt	Leight

Equipement

Picture

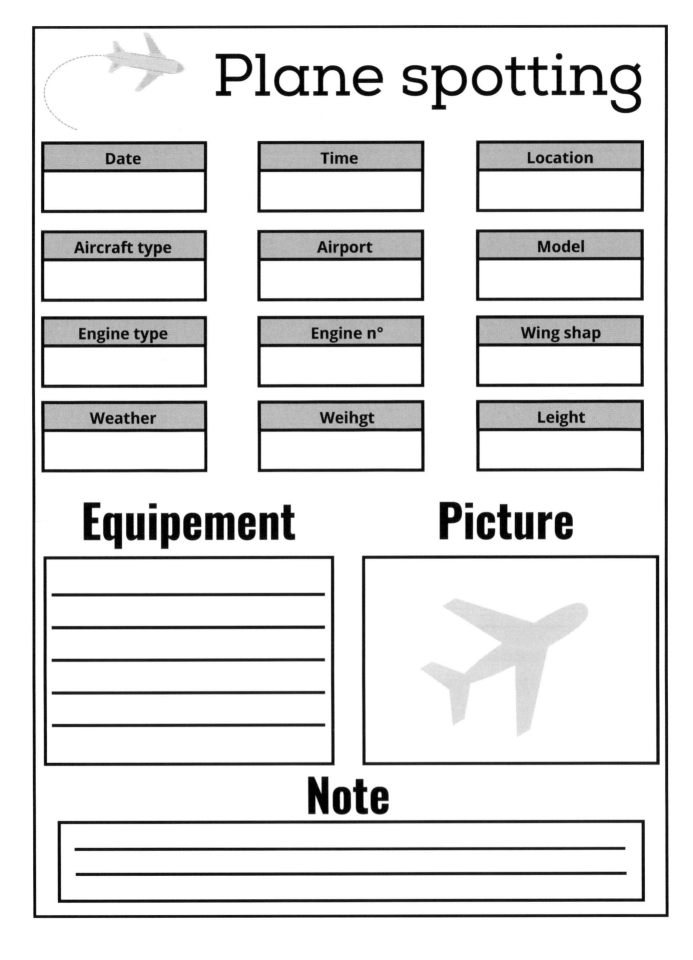

Note

Plane spotting

Date	Time	Location

Aircraft type	Airport	Model

Engine type	Engine n°	Wing shap

Weather	Weihgt	Leight

Equipement

Picture

Note

Plane spotting

Date	Time	Location

Aircraft type	Airport	Model

Engine type	Engine n°	Wing shap

Weather	Weihgt	Leight

Equipement

Picture

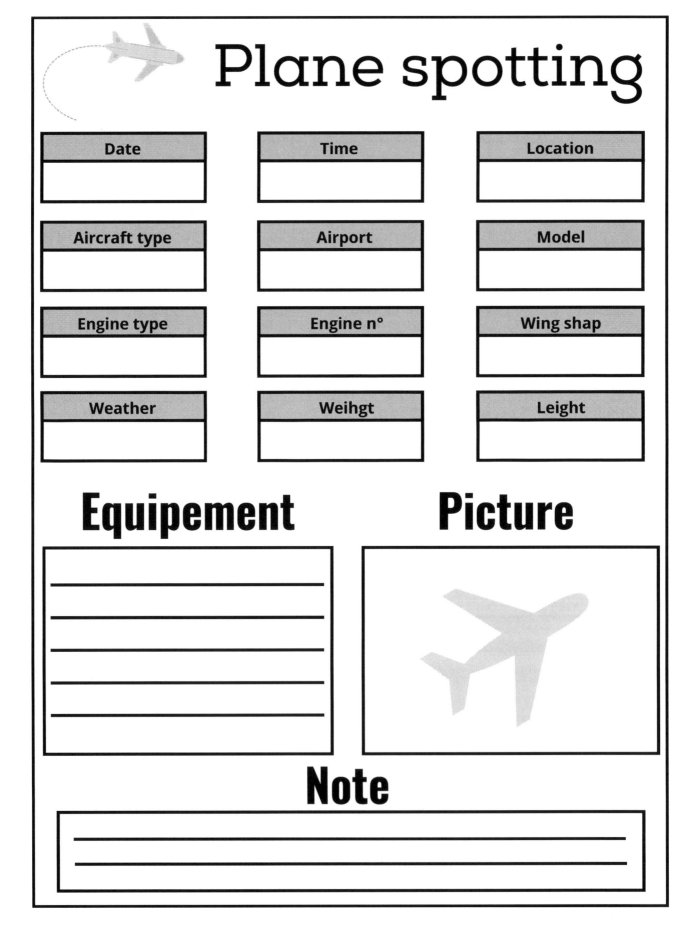

Note

Plane spotting

Date	Time	Location

Aircraft type	Airport	Model

Engine type	Engine n°	Wing shap

Weather	Weihgt	Leight

Equipement

Picture

Note

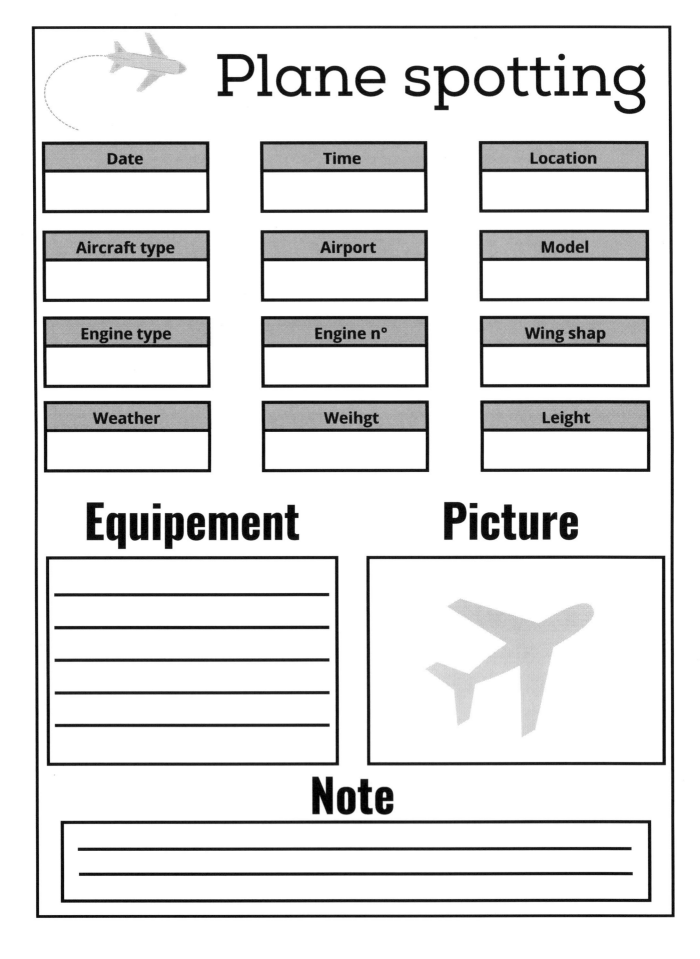

Plane spotting

Date	Time	Location

Aircraft type	Airport	Model

Engine type	Engine n°	Wing shap

Weather	Weihgt	Leight

Equipement

Picture

Note

Plane spotting

Date	Time	Location

Aircraft type	Airport	Model

Engine type	Engine n°	Wing shap

Weather	Weihgt	Leight

Equipement

Picture

Note

Plane spotting

Date	Time	Location

Aircraft type	Airport	Model

Engine type	Engine n°	Wing shap

Weather	Weihgt	Leight

Equipement

Picture

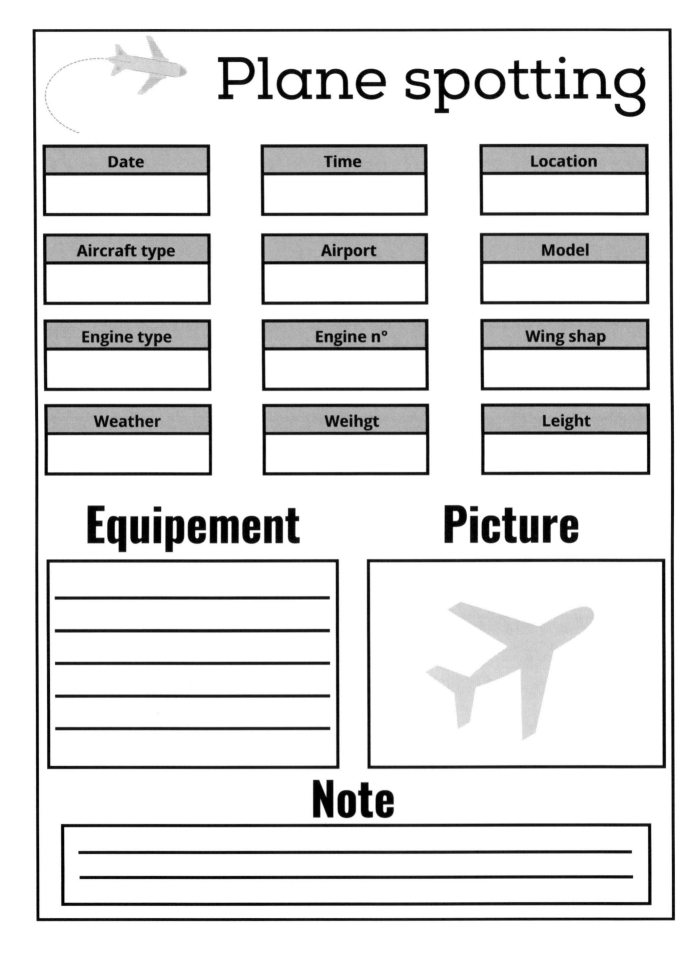

Note

Plane spotting

Date	Time	Location

Aircraft type	Airport	Model

Engine type	Engine n°	Wing shap

Weather	Weihgt	Leight

Equipement

Picture

Note

Plane spotting

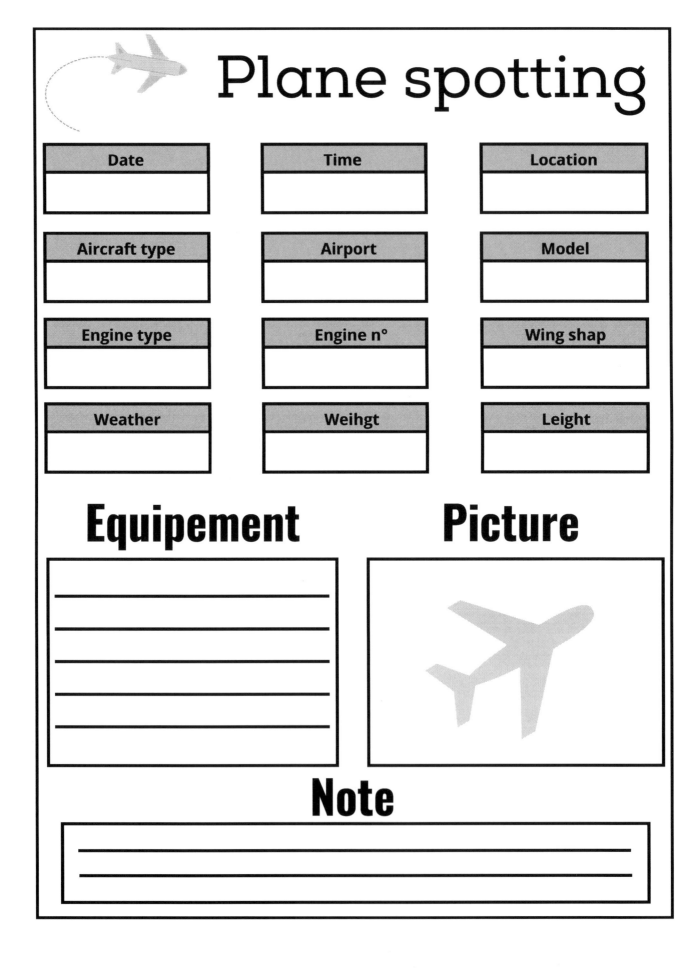

Date	Time	Location

Aircraft type	Airport	Model

Engine type	Engine n°	Wing shap

Weather	Weihgt	Leight

Equipement

Picture

Note

Plane spotting

Date	Time	Location

Aircraft type	Airport	Model

Engine type	Engine n°	Wing shap

Weather	Weihgt	Leight

Equipement

Picture

Note

Plane spotting

Date	Time	Location

Aircraft type	Airport	Model

Engine type	Engine n°	Wing shap

Weather	Weihgt	Leight

Equipement

Picture

Note

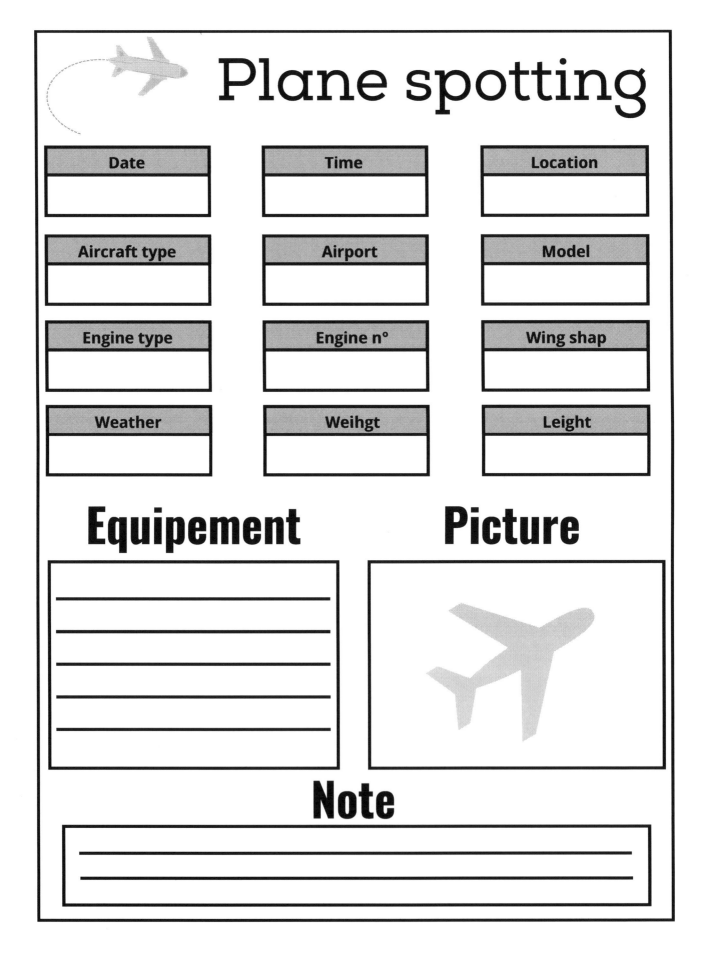

Plane spotting

Date	Time	Location

Aircraft type	Airport	Model

Engine type	Engine n°	Wing shap

Weather	Weihgt	Leight

Equipement

Picture

Note

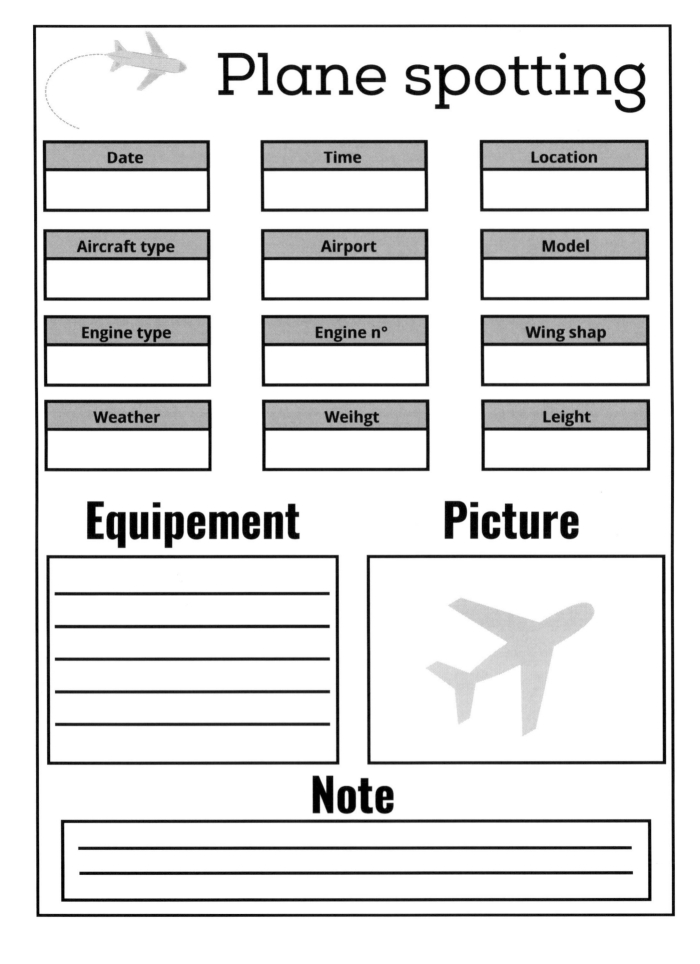

Plane spotting

Date	Time	Location

Aircraft type	Airport	Model

Engine type	Engine n°	Wing shap

Weather	Weihgt	Leight

Equipement

Picture

Note

Plane spotting

Date	Time	Location

Aircraft type	Airport	Model

Engine type	Engine n°	Wing shap

Weather	Weihgt	Leight

Equipement

Picture

Note

Plane spotting

Date	Time	Location

Aircraft type	Airport	Model

Engine type	Engine n°	Wing shap

Weather	Weihgt	Leight

Equipement

Picture

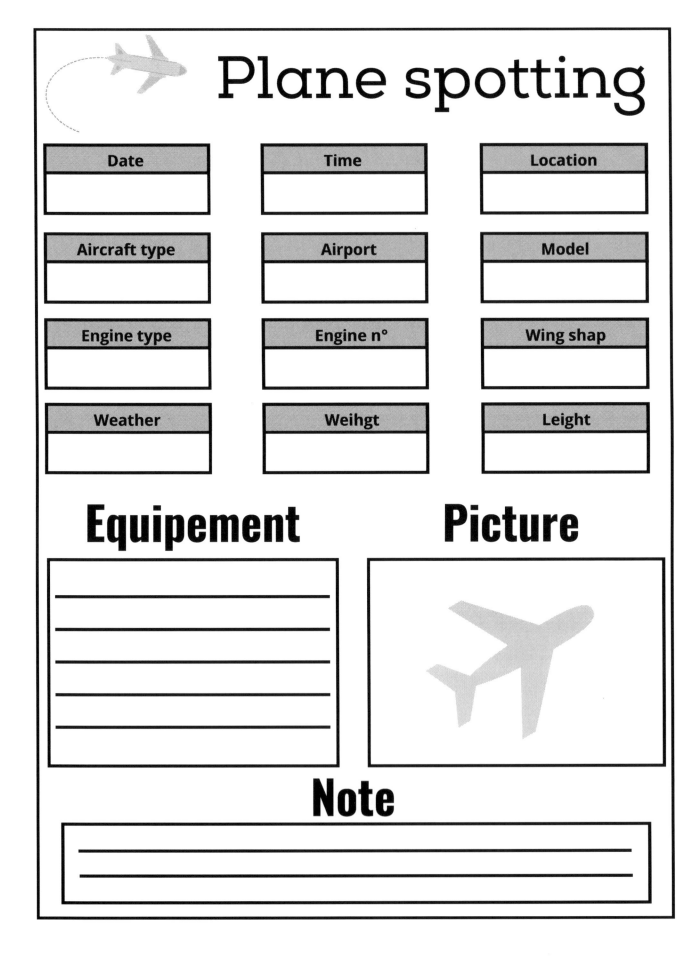

Note

Plane spotting

Date	Time	Location

Aircraft type	Airport	Model

Engine type	Engine n°	Wing shap

Weather	Weihgt	Leight

Equipement

Picture

Note

Plane spotting

Date	Time	Location

Aircraft type	Airport	Model

Engine type	Engine n°	Wing shap

Weather	Weihgt	Leight

Equipement

Picture

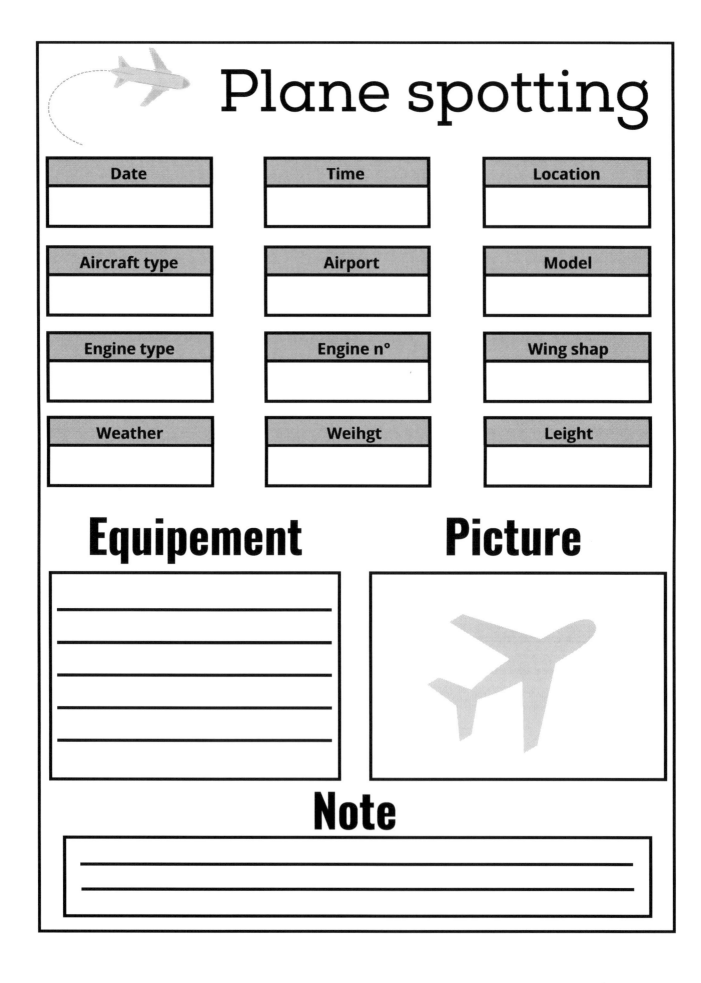

Note

Plane spotting

Date	Time	Location

Aircraft type	Airport	Model

Engine type	Engine n°	Wing shap

Weather	Weihgt	Leight

Equipement

Picture

Note

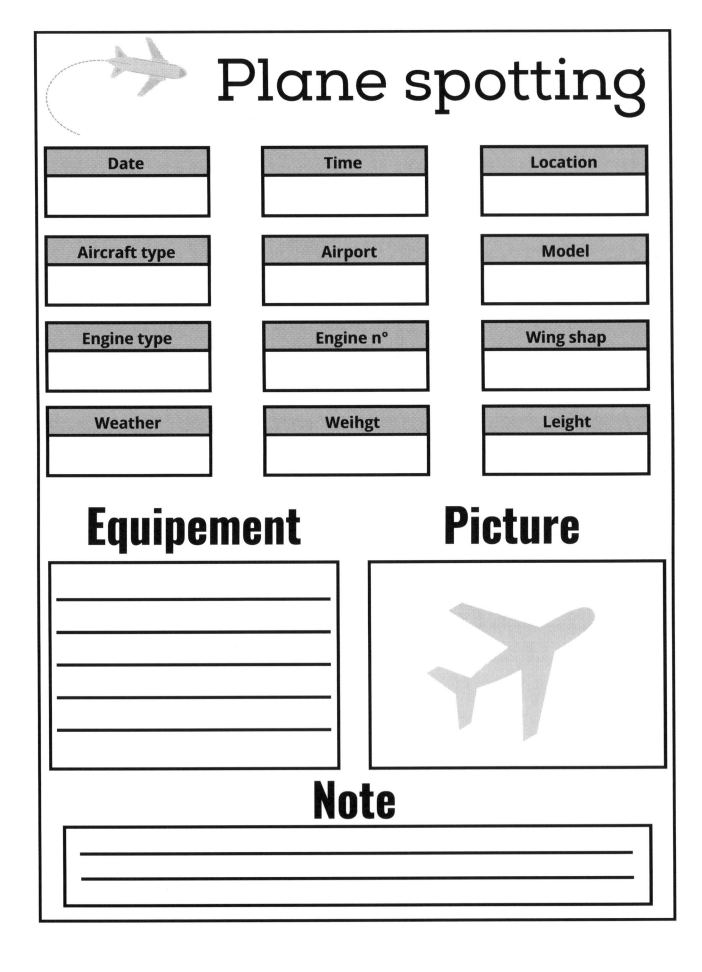

Plane spotting

Date	Time	Location

Aircraft type	Airport	Model

Engine type	Engine n°	Wing shap

Weather	Weihgt	Leight

Equipement

Picture

Note

Plane spotting

Date	Time	Location

Aircraft type	Airport	Model

Engine type	Engine n°	Wing shap

Weather	Weihgt	Leight

Equipement

Picture

Note

Plane spotting

Date	Time	Location

Aircraft type	Airport	Model

Engine type	Engine n°	Wing shap

Weather	Weihgt	Leight

Equipement

Picture

Note

Plane spotting

Date	Time	Location

Aircraft type	Airport	Model

Engine type	Engine n°	Wing shap

Weather	Weihgt	Leight

Equipement

Picture

Note

Plane spotting

Date	Time	Location

Aircraft type	Airport	Model

Engine type	Engine n°	Wing shap

Weather	Weihgt	Leight

Equipement

Picture

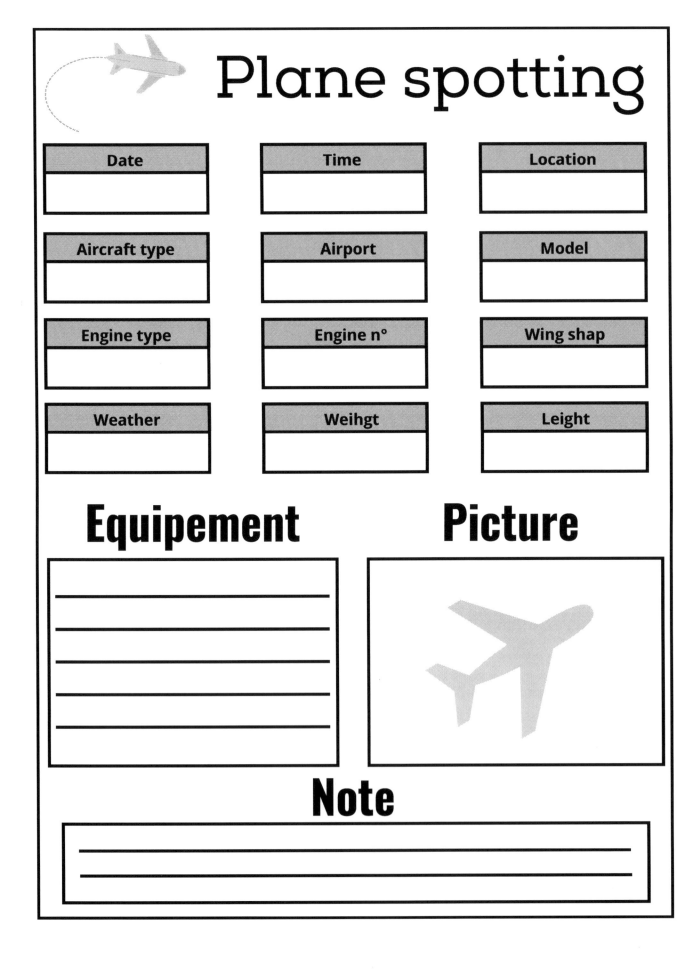

Note

Plane spotting

Date	Time	Location

Aircraft type	Airport	Model

Engine type	Engine n°	Wing shap

Weather	Weihgt	Leight

Equipement

Picture

Note

Plane spotting

Date	Time	Location

Aircraft type	Airport	Model

Engine type	Engine n°	Wing shap

Weather	Weihgt	Leight

Equipement

Picture

Note

Plane spotting

Date	Time	Location

Aircraft type	Airport	Model

Engine type	Engine n°	Wing shap

Weather	Weihgt	Leight

Equipement

Picture

Note

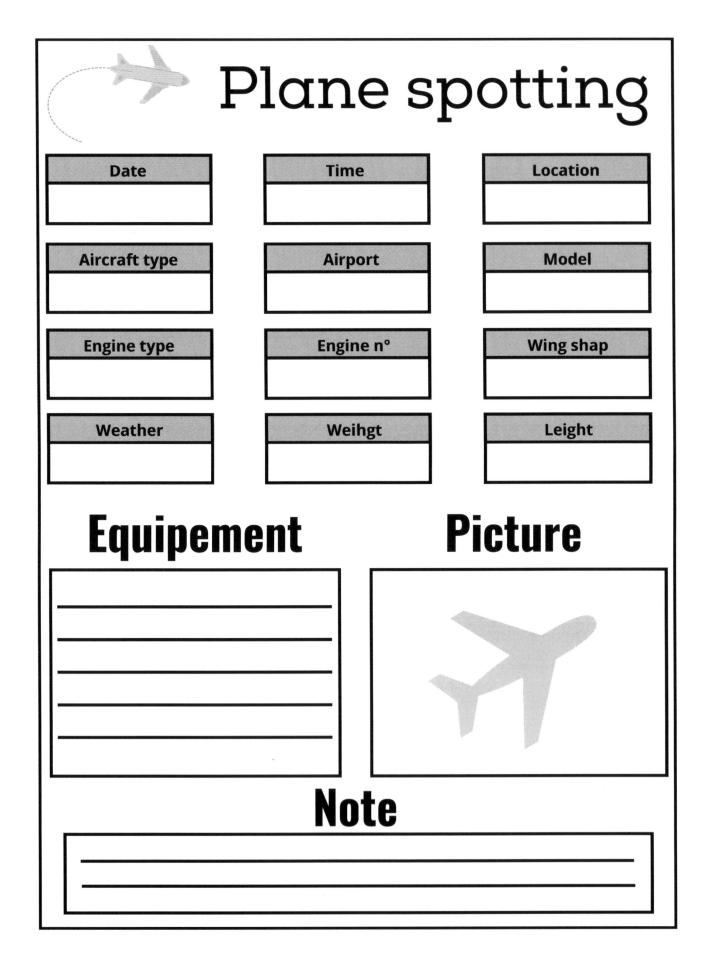

Plane spotting

Date		Time		Location	

Aircraft type		Airport		Model	

Engine type		Engine n°		Wing shap	

Weather		Weihgt		Leight	

Equipement

Picture

Note

Plane spotting

Date	Time	Location

Aircraft type	Airport	Model

Engine type	Engine n°	Wing shap

Weather	Weihgt	Leight

Equipement

Picture

Note

Plane spotting

Date	Time	Location

Aircraft type	Airport	Model

Engine type	Engine n°	Wing shap

Weather	Weihgt	Leight

Equipement

Picture

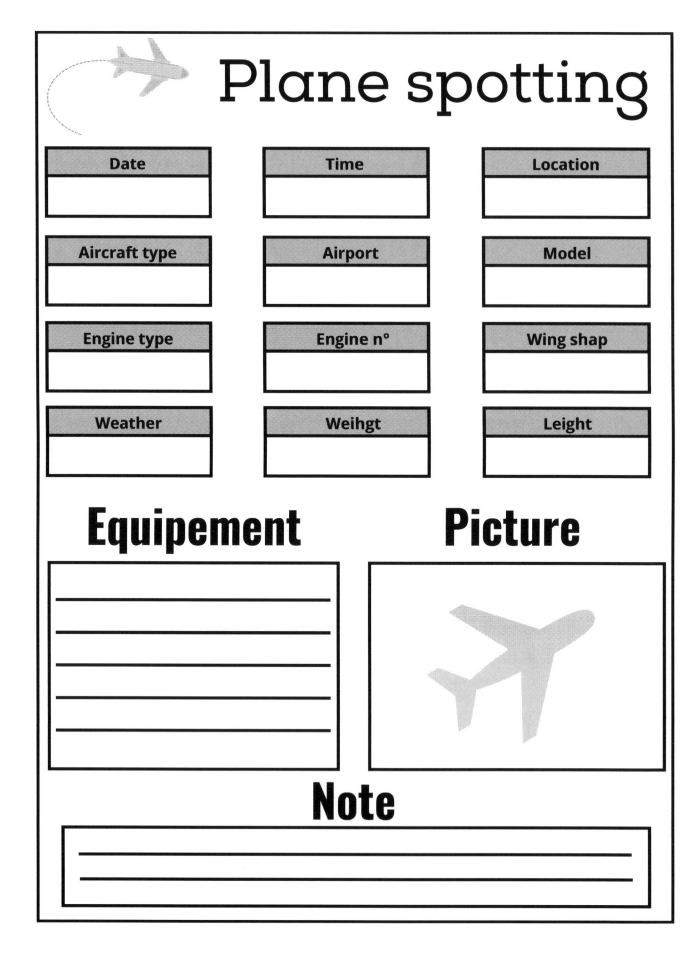

Note

Plane spotting

Date	Time	Location

Aircraft type	Airport	Model

Engine type	Engine n°	Wing shap

Weather	Weihgt	Leight

Equipement

Picture

Note

Plane spotting

Date	Time	Location

Aircraft type	Airport	Model

Engine type	Engine n°	Wing shap

Weather	Weihgt	Leight

Equipement

Picture

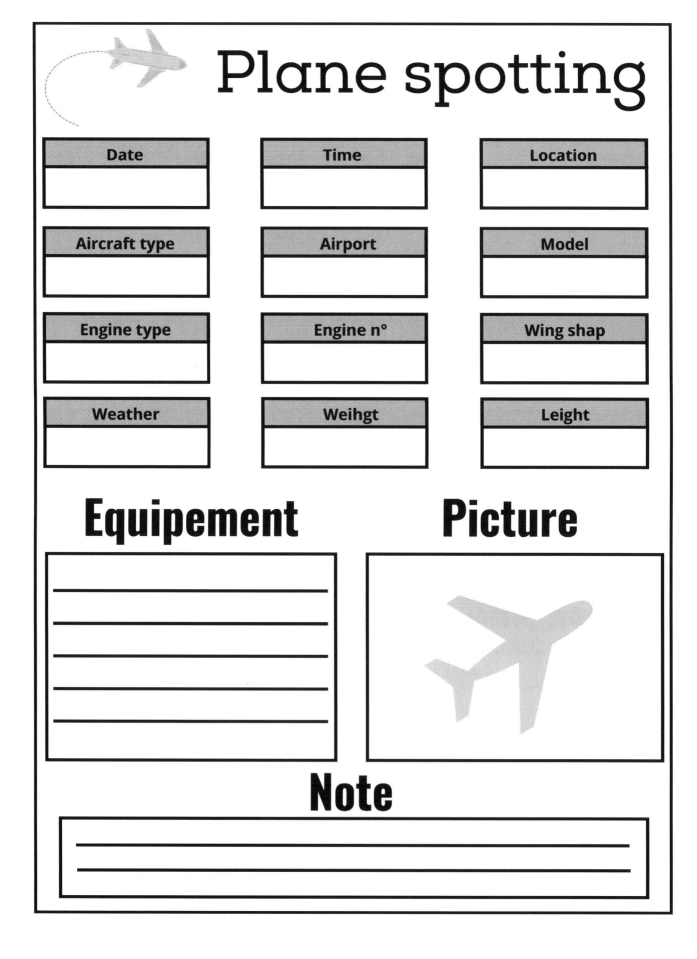

Note

Plane spotting

Date	Time	Location

Aircraft type	Airport	Model

Engine type	Engine n°	Wing shap

Weather	Weihgt	Leight

Equipement

Picture

Note

Plane spotting

Date	Time	Location

Aircraft type	Airport	Model

Engine type	Engine n°	Wing shap

Weather	Weihgt	Leight

Equipement

Picture

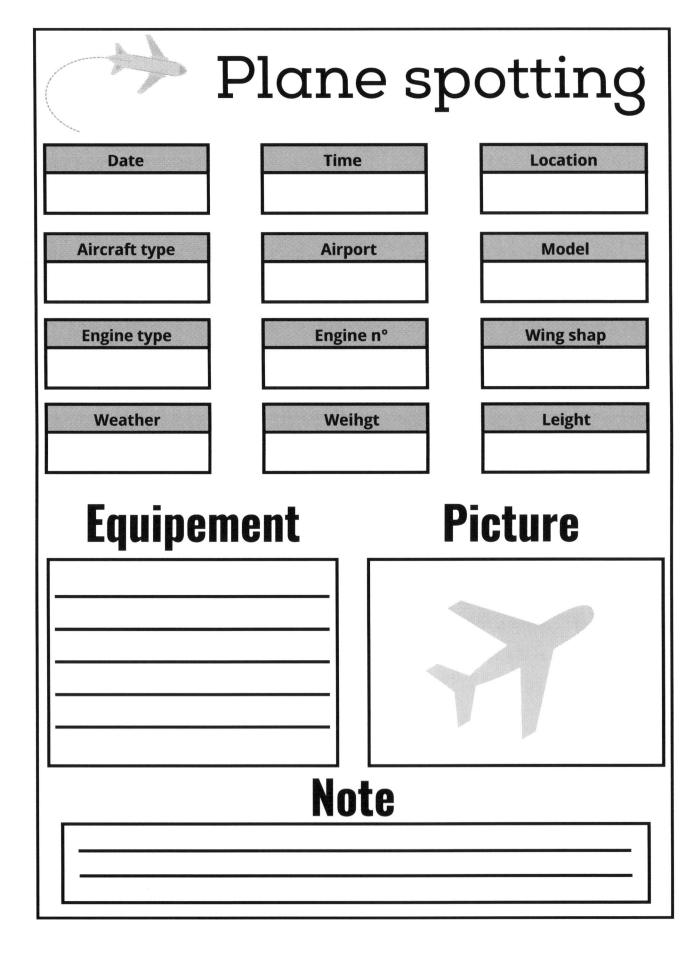

Note

Plane spotting

Date	Time	Location

Aircraft type	Airport	Model

Engine type	Engine n°	Wing shap

Weather	Weihgt	Leight

Equipement

Picture

Note

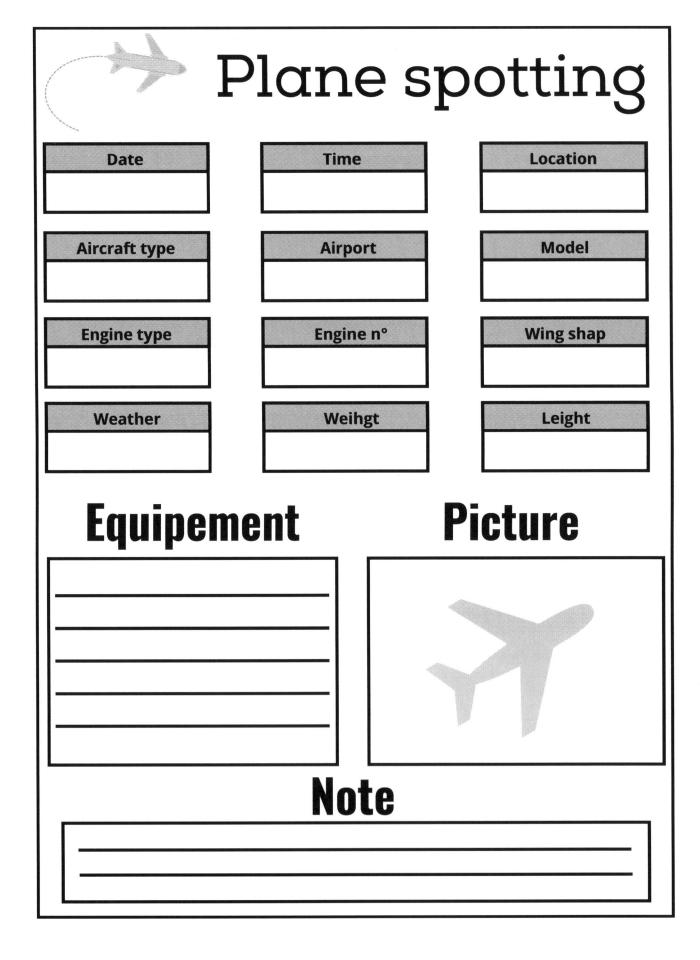

Plane spotting

Date	Time	Location

Aircraft type	Airport	Model

Engine type	Engine n°	Wing shap

Weather	Weihgt	Leight

Equipement

Picture

Note

Plane spotting

Date	Time	Location

Aircraft type	Airport	Model

Engine type	Engine n°	Wing shap

Weather	Weihgt	Leight

Equipement

Picture

Note

Plane spotting

Date	Time	Location

Aircraft type	Airport	Model

Engine type	Engine n°	Wing shap

Weather	Weihgt	Leight

Equipement

Picture

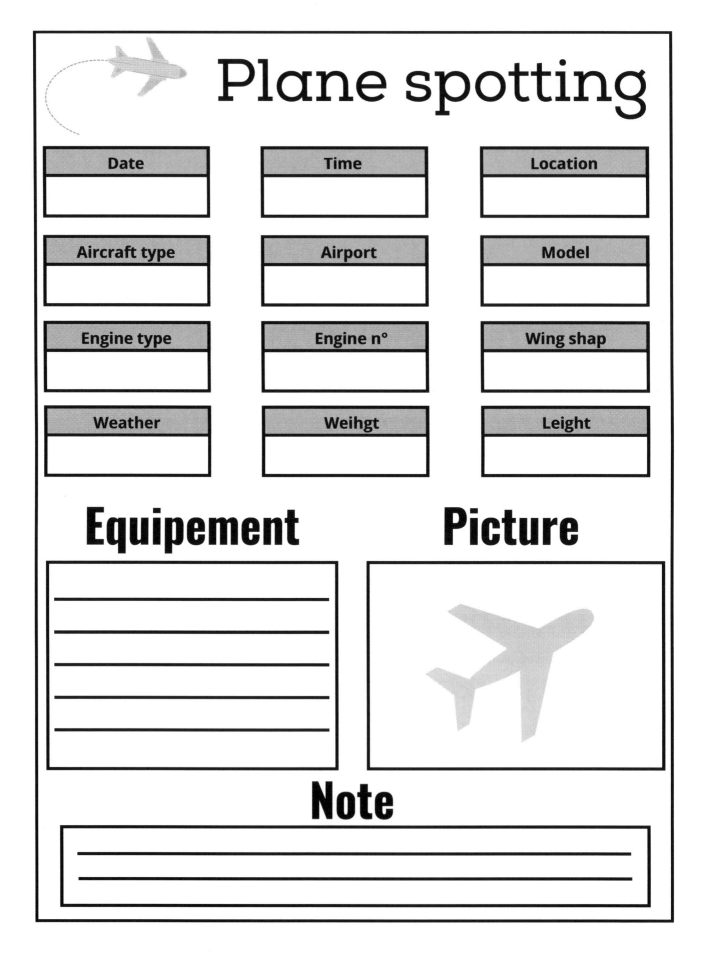

Note

Plane spotting

Date	Time	Location

Aircraft type	Airport	Model

Engine type	Engine n°	Wing shap

Weather	Weihgt	Leight

Equipement

Picture

Note

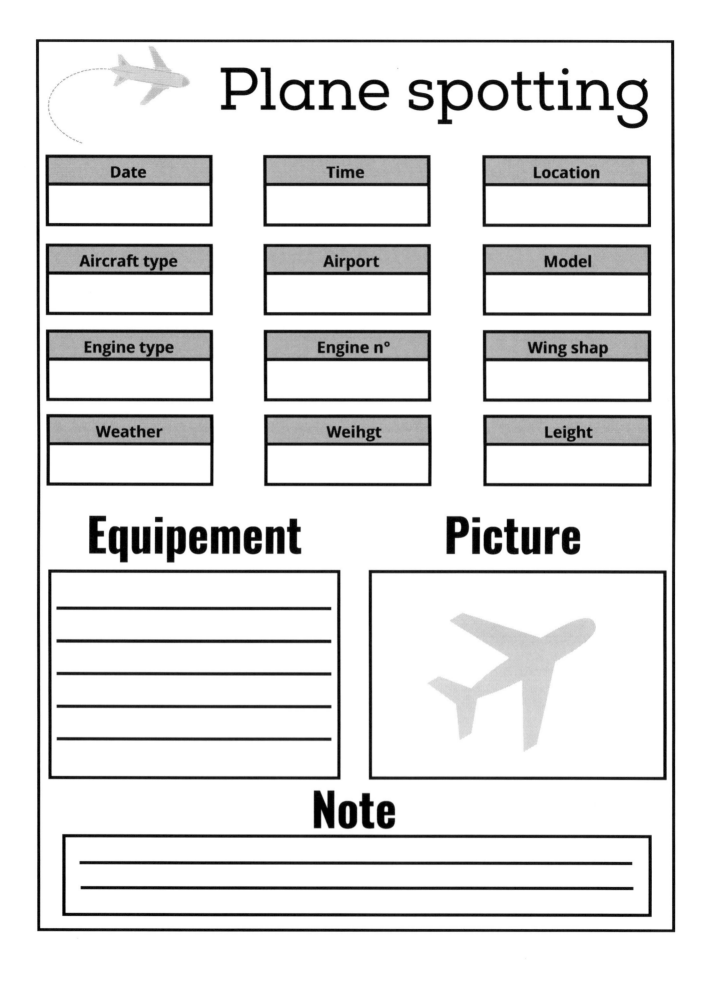

Plane spotting

Date	Time	Location

Aircraft type	Airport	Model

Engine type	Engine n°	Wing shap

Weather	Weihgt	Leight

Equipement

Picture

Note

Plane spotting

Date	Time	Location

Aircraft type	Airport	Model

Engine type	Engine n°	Wing shap

Weather	Weihgt	Leight

Equipement

Picture

Note

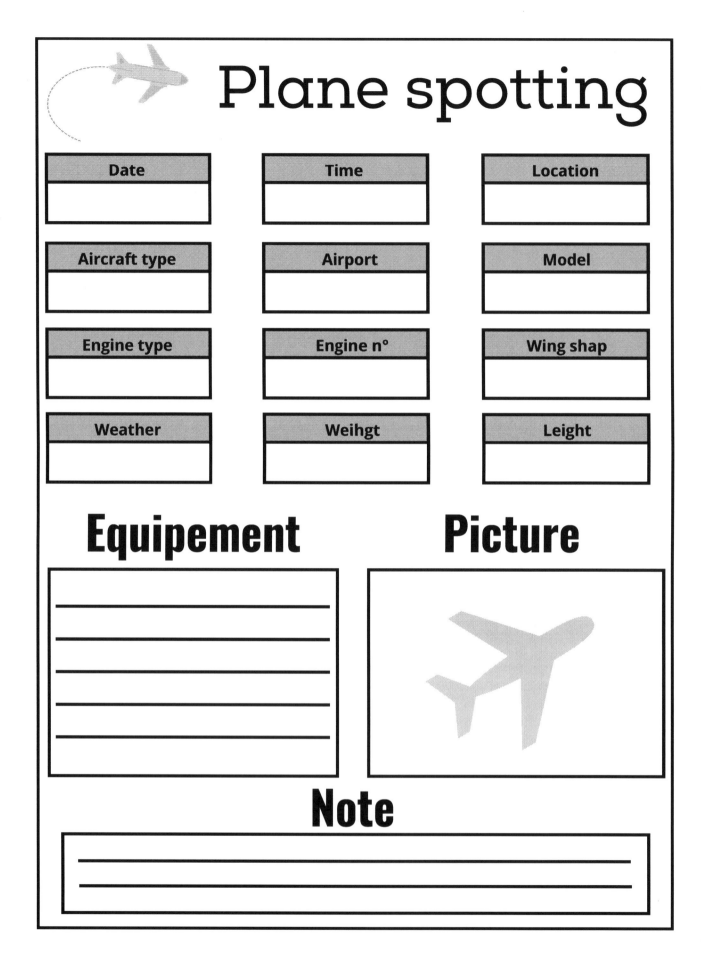

Plane spotting

Date	Time	Location

Aircraft type	Airport	Model

Engine type	Engine n°	Wing shap

Weather	Weihgt	Leight

Equipement

Picture

Note

Plane spotting

Date	Time	Location

Aircraft type	Airport	Model

Engine type	Engine n°	Wing shap

Weather	Weihgt	Leight

Equipement

Picture

Note

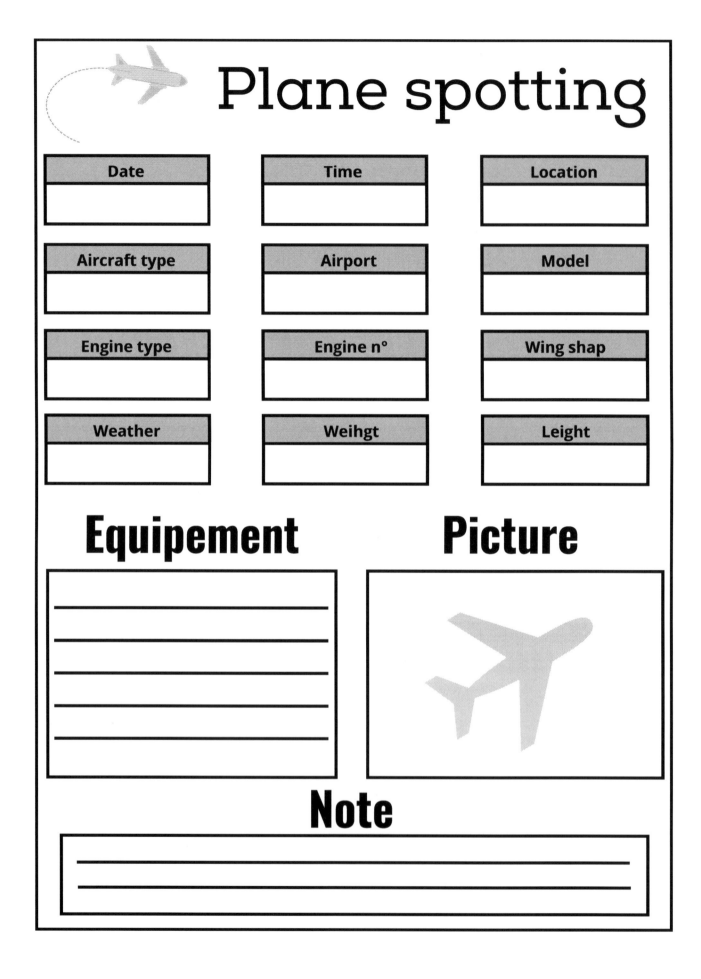

Plane spotting

Date	Time	Location

Aircraft type	Airport	Model

Engine type	Engine n°	Wing shap

Weather	Weihgt	Leight

Equipement

Picture

Note

Plane spotting

Date	Time	Location

Aircraft type	Airport	Model

Engine type	Engine n°	Wing shap

Weather	Weihgt	Leight

Equipement

Picture

Note

Plane spotting

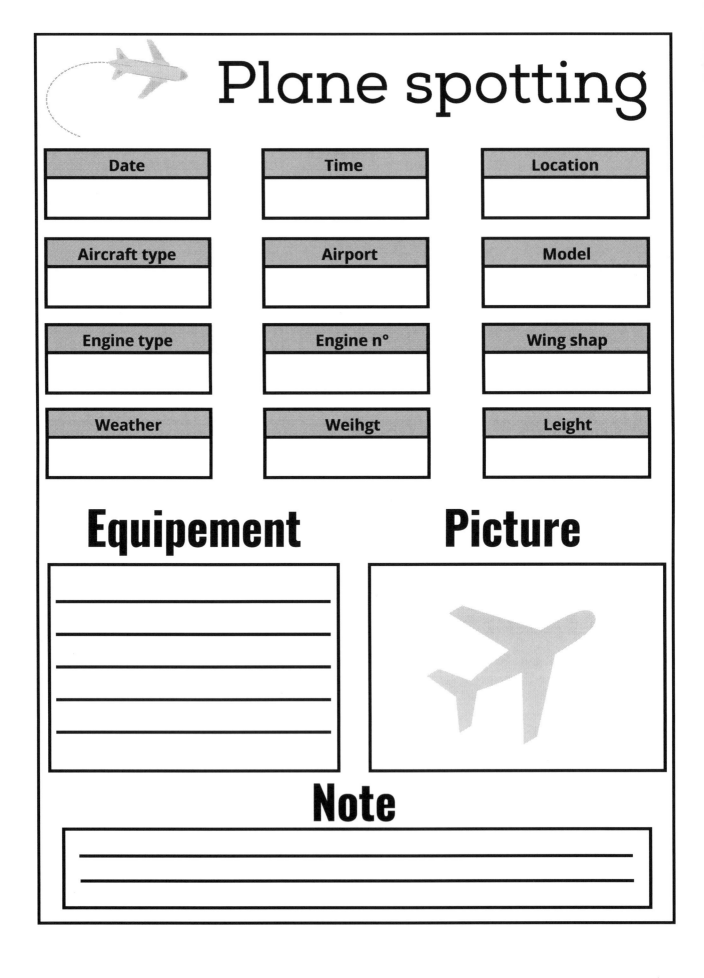

Date	Time	Location

Aircraft type	Airport	Model

Engine type	Engine n°	Wing shap

Weather	Weihgt	Leight

Equipement

Picture

Note

Plane spotting

Date	Time	Location

Aircraft type	Airport	Model

Engine type	Engine n°	Wing shap

Weather	Weihgt	Leight

Equipement

Picture

Note

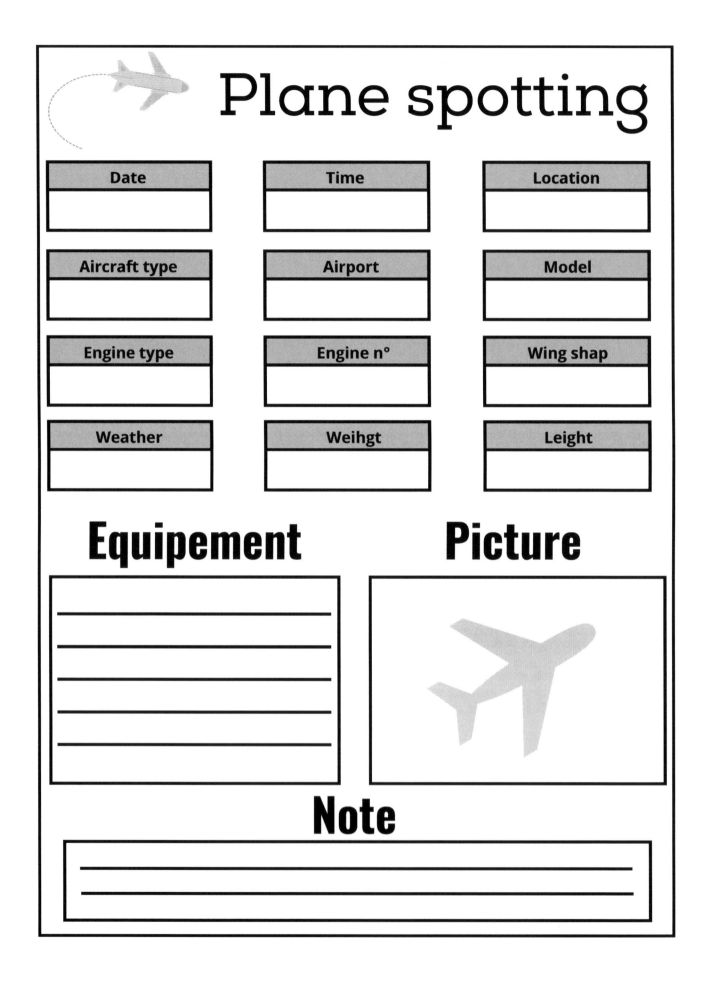

Plane spotting

Date	Time	Location

Aircraft type	Airport	Model

Engine type	Engine n°	Wing shap

Weather	Weihgt	Leight

Equipement

Picture

Note

Plane spotting

Date	Time	Location

Aircraft type	Airport	Model

Engine type	Engine n°	Wing shap

Weather	Weihgt	Leight

Equipement

Picture

Note

Plane spotting

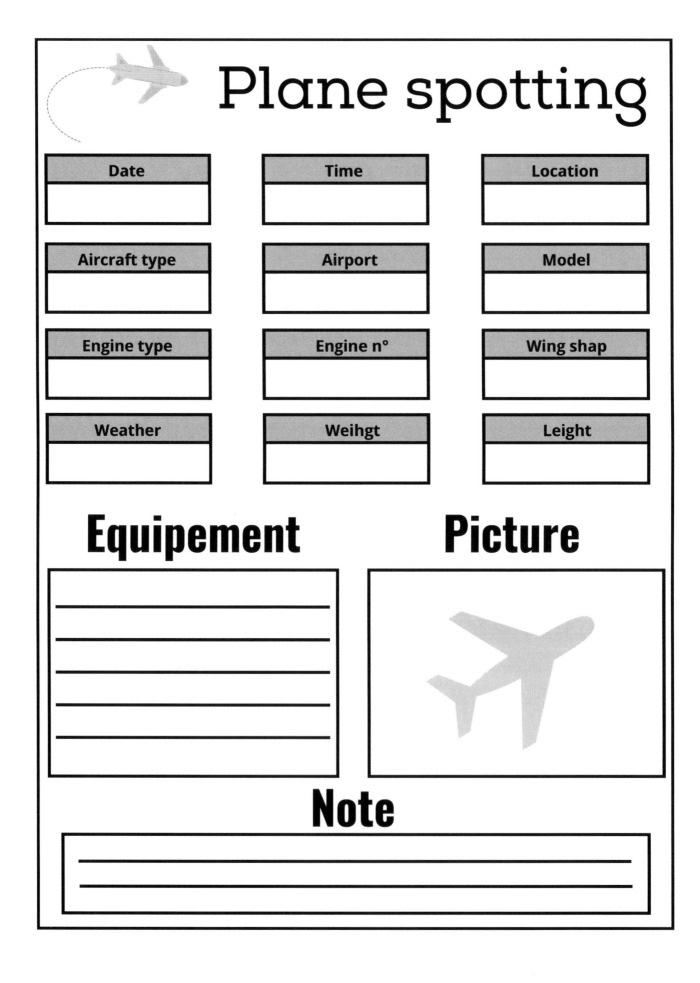

Date	Time	Location

Aircraft type	Airport	Model

Engine type	Engine n°	Wing shap

Weather	Weihgt	Leight

Equipement

Picture

Note

Plane spotting

Date	Time	Location

Aircraft type	Airport	Model

Engine type	Engine n°	Wing shap

Weather	Weihgt	Leight

Equipement

Picture

Note

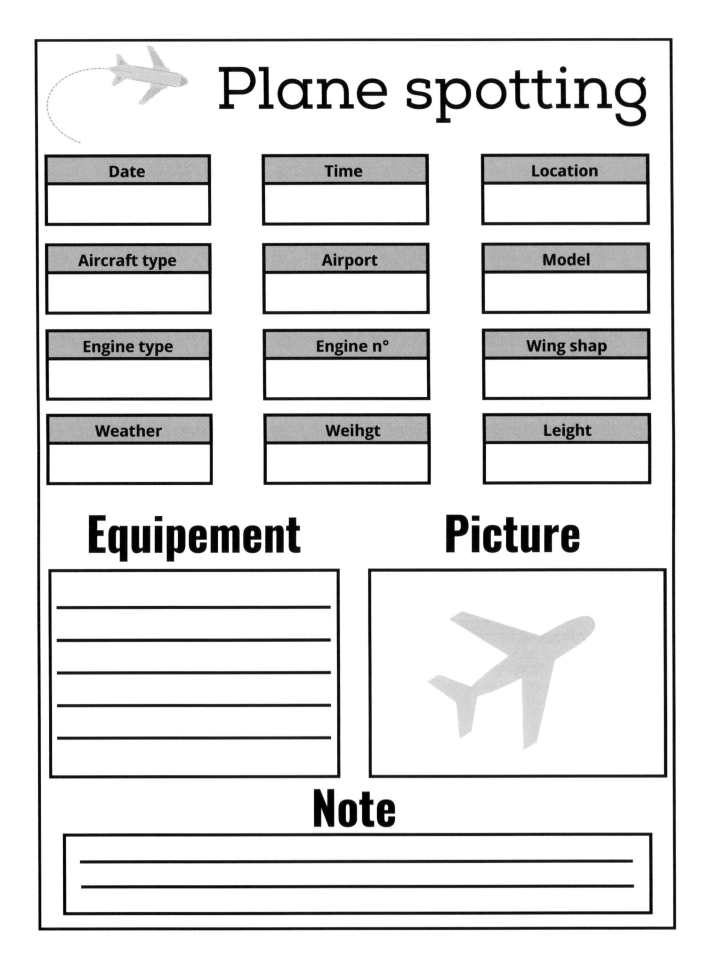

Plane spotting

Date	Time	Location

Aircraft type	Airport	Model

Engine type	Engine n°	Wing shap

Weather	Weihgt	Leight

Equipement

Picture

Note

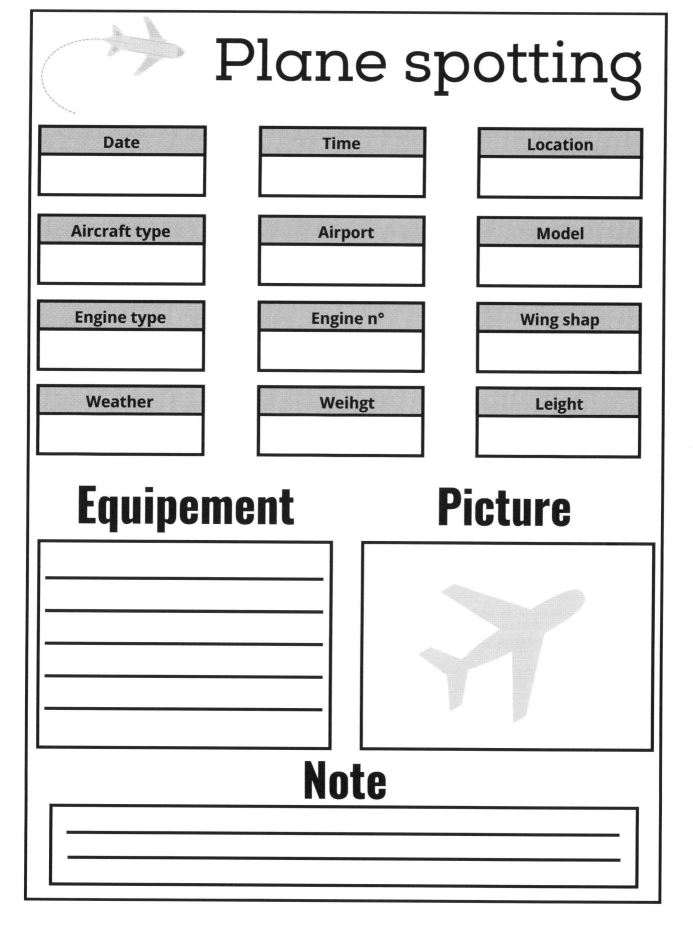

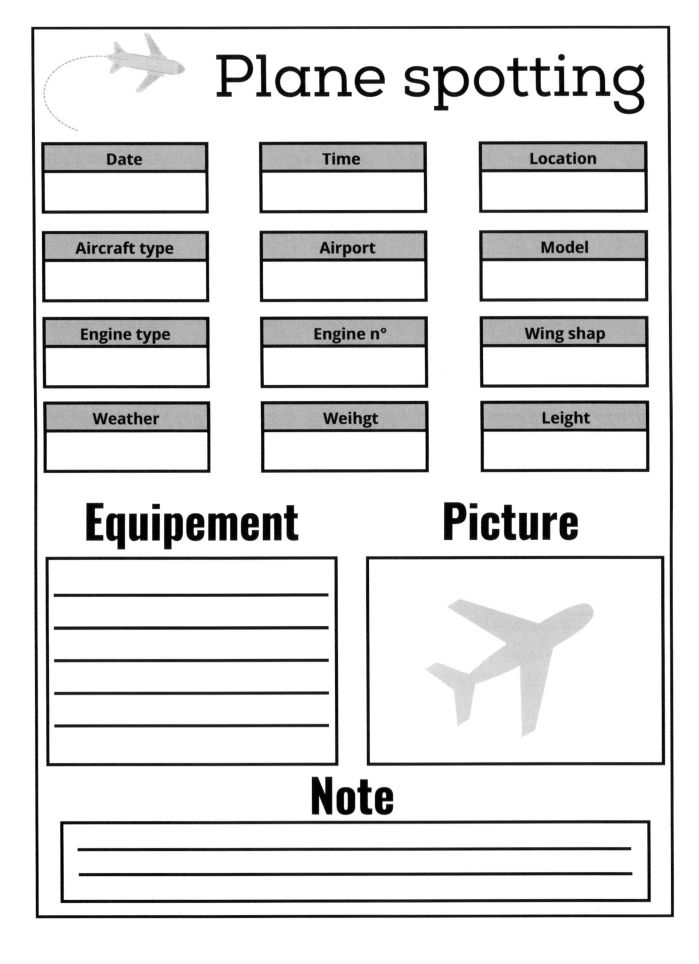

Plane spotting

Date	Time	Location

Aircraft type	Airport	Model

Engine type	Engine n°	Wing shap

Weather	Weihgt	Leight

Equipement

Picture

Note

Plane spotting

Date	Time	Location

Aircraft type	Airport	Model

Engine type	Engine n°	Wing shap

Weather	Weihgt	Leight

Equipement

Picture

Note

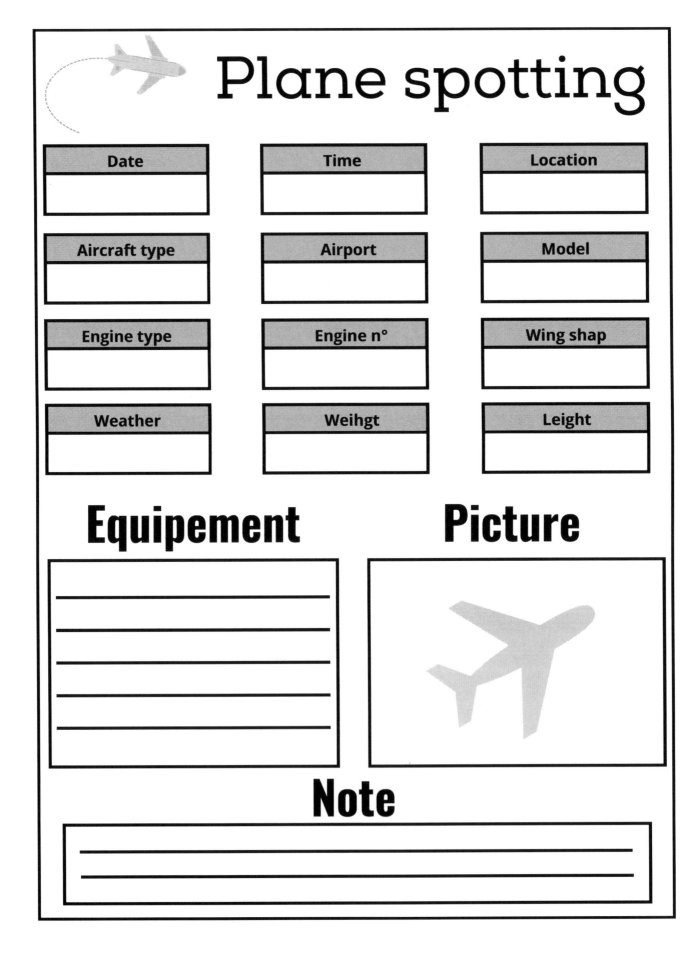

Plane spotting

Date	Time	Location

Aircraft type	Airport	Model

Engine type	Engine n°	Wing shap

Weather	Weihgt	Leight

Equipement

Picture

Note

Plane spotting

Date	Time	Location

Aircraft type	Airport	Model

Engine type	Engine n°	Wing shap

Weather	Weihgt	Leight

Equipement

Picture

Note

Plane spotting

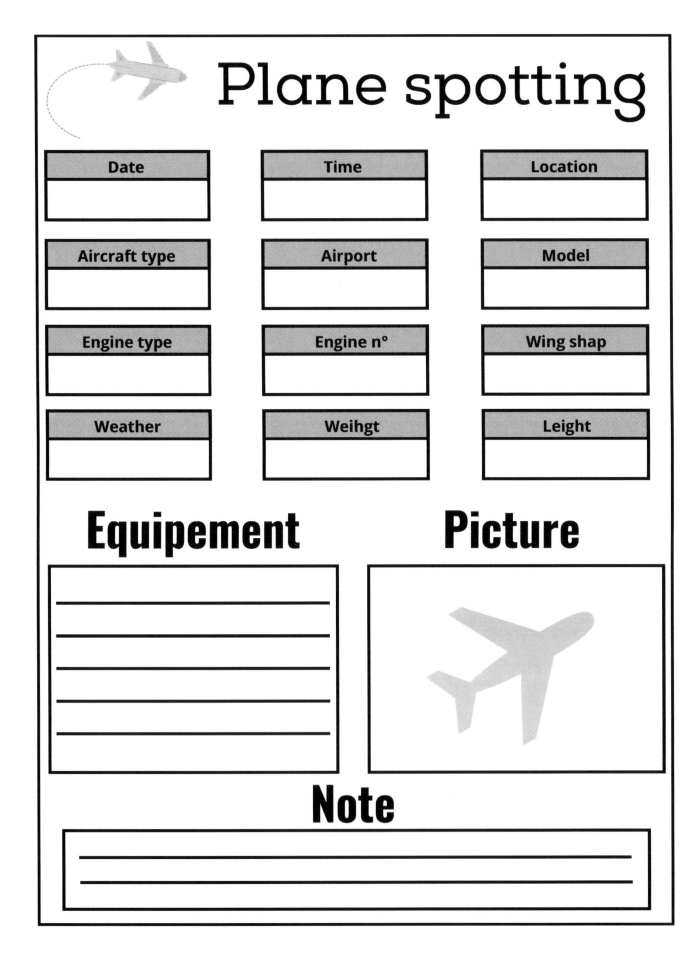

Date	Time	Location

Aircraft type	Airport	Model

Engine type	Engine n°	Wing shap

Weather	Weihgt	Leight

Equipement

Picture

Note

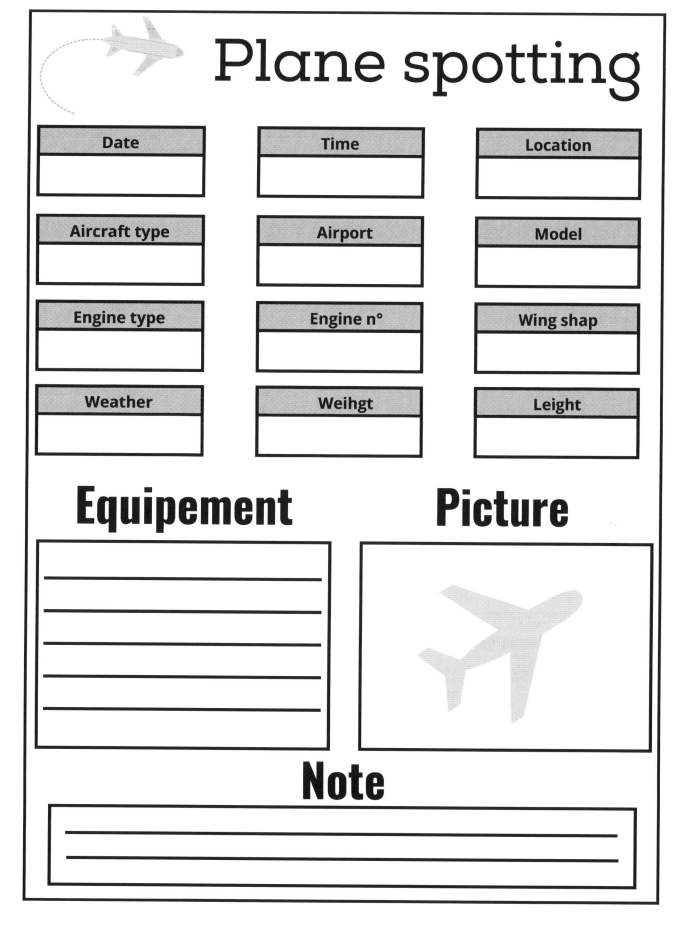

Plane spotting

Date	Time	Location

Aircraft type	Airport	Model

Engine type	Engine n°	Wing shap

Weather	Weihgt	Leight

Equipement

Picture

Note

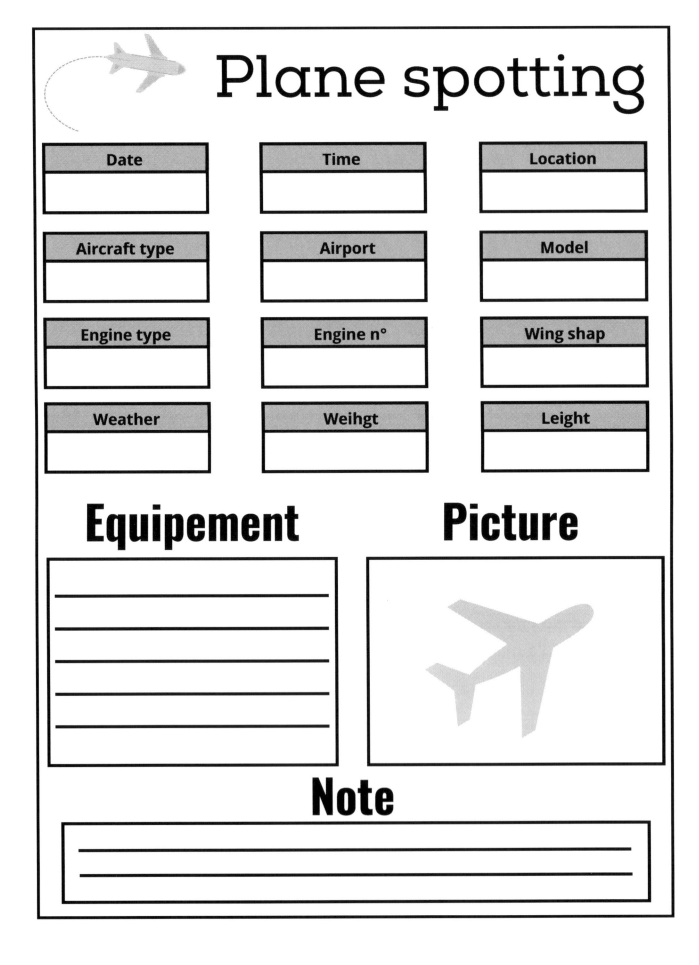

Plane spotting

Date	Time	Location

Aircraft type	Airport	Model

Engine type	Engine n°	Wing shap

Weather	Weihgt	Leight

Equipement

Picture

Note

Plane spotting

Date	Time	Location

Aircraft type	Airport	Model

Engine type	Engine n°	Wing shap

Weather	Weihgt	Leight

Equipement

Picture

Note

Plane spotting

Date	Time	Location

Aircraft type	Airport	Model

Engine type	Engine n°	Wing shap

Weather	Weihgt	Leight

Equipement

Picture

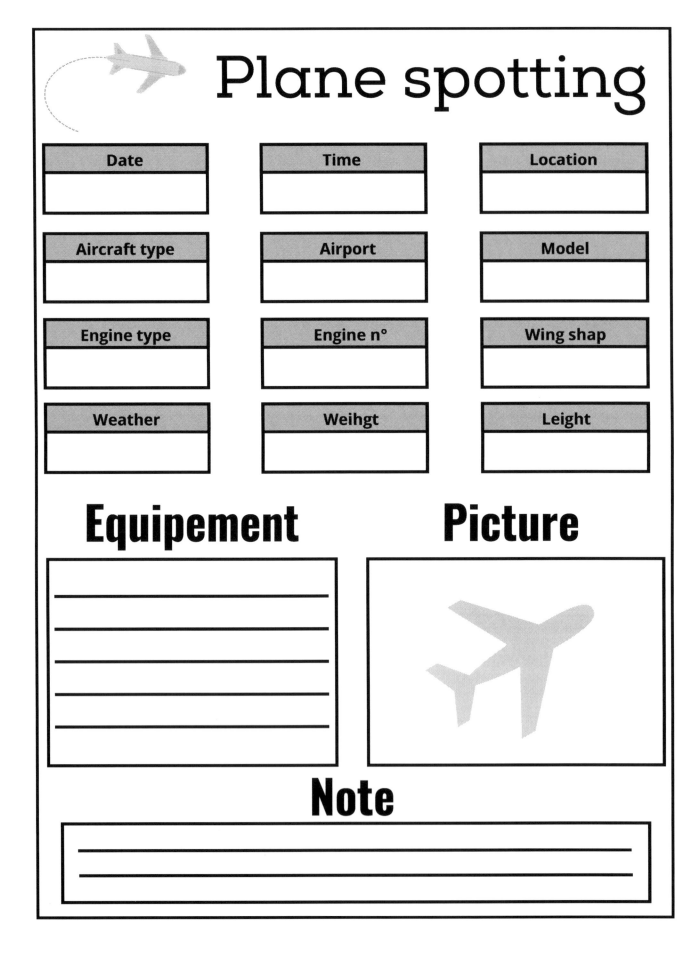

Note

Printed in Great Britain
by Amazon